Second Edition, Copyright © 2014, 2015, 2017
ISBN: 978-1-312-74639-8

All rights reserved. No part of this publication may be reproduced, distributed, or transmitted in any form or by any means, including photocopying, recording, or other electronic or mechanical methods, without the prior written permission of the publisher, except in the case of brief quotations embodied in critical reviews and certain other noncommercial uses permitted by copyright law. For permission requests, write to:

Tuleyome
607 North Street
Woodland, CA 95695

This species guide contains photographs and information on over 200 distinct species of plants and animals, but they still only comprise a tiny fraction of the flora and fauna found throughout the Berryessa Snow Mountain region. While the guide is not comprehensive, it provides an introduction to the diversity of life found in this rich area, including many common as well as endangered species.

You will see the words "endemic to California" throughout this guide. This term means that the animal, insect or plant is "limited" to California: *found in California and nowhere else in the world.*

Tuleyome is a 501(c)(3) nonprofit conservation organization based in Woodland, California which spearheaded the campaign that established the Berryessa Snow Mountain National Monument. All donations are tax deductible.

Tuleyome
607 North Street, Woodland, CA 95695
Website: www.tuleyome.org
Facebook: https://www.facebook.com/Tuleyome
Twitter: http://www.twitter.com/tuleyomeorg
Website: www. berryessasnowmountain.org

This guide was compiled by Certified California Naturalist and photographer Mary K. Hanson. We thank photographers Andrew Borcher, Andrew Fulks, Bob Sikora, Charlotte Orr, Cherilyn Burton, Doug Donaldson, Hartmut Wisch, Jake Ruygt, Jennifer L. Kalt, Jim Rose, John Game, J. N. Stuart, Roger Jones, Ron Dudley, Sam Murray, Sangeet Khalsa, Silvia Wright, Terry England, Wendy E. Miller, and others for their wonderful photographs. We also thank our volunteer editors, Katherine Mawdsley and Christina Mann, as well as Aaron E. Simms and the California Native Plant Society for their expertise.

All photos in this guide are used with permission.
Photographers may retain all or some of their rights.

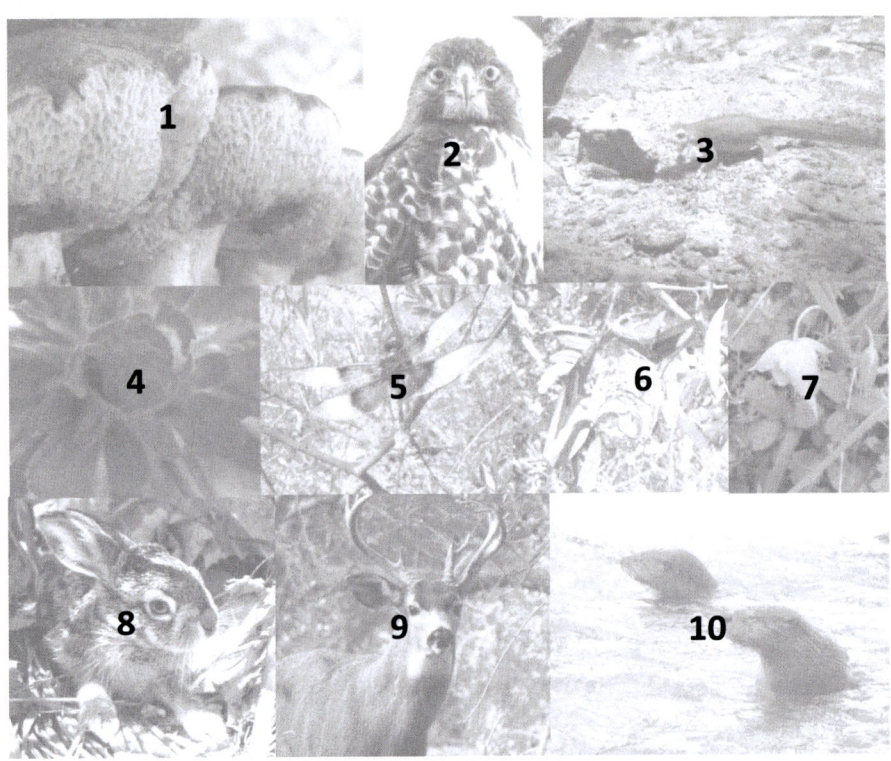

Cover Art: (1) Bolete Mushrooms by Mary K. Hanson; (2) Red-Tailed Hawk by Dough Donaldson; (3) California Newt by Andrew Fulks; (4) Indian Warrior by Jim Rose; (5) Widow Skimmer Dragonfly by Mary K. Hanson; (6) Hoary Bat by Roger Jones; (7) Fairy Lantern by Mary K. Hanson; (8) Jackrabbit Leveret by Roger Jones; (9) Columbian Black-Tailed Mule Deer by Mary K. Hanson; (10) River Otters by Bob Schneider.

Table of Contents

	Page
Establishment of the Berryessa Snow Mountain National Monument	4
Federal and State of California Conservation Status Keys	8
NatureServe Ranking System	9
California Native Plant Society Plant Ranking System	9
Fauna:	11
Birds	12
Insects	34
Common Wasp Galls	49
Mammals	50
Reptiles, Fish, Amphibians	60
Plants:	67
Flowers and Plants Listed by Color	68
Flowers, Plants and Grasses	70
Trees	101
Fungus and Lichen	117
Common Slime Molds	122
Habitat Systems within the Berryessa Snow Mountain Region	123
Citizen Science: How You Can Help Scientists Track Species throughout the Berryessa Snow Mountain Region	124
Sources and Acknowledgments for the Species Guide	126
How You Can Help Restore Areas in the Berryessa Snow Mountain Region Damaged by the Wild Fires of 2015	128
Associated Essays:	129
Scientific and Conservation Values of the Berryessa Snow Mountain Region	130
The Berryessa-Snow Mountain Region: Its Remarkable Geologic Features	132
Protecting Water Quality and Supply And Restoring Resilient Forests in the Berryessa Snow Mountain National Monument	134

Establishment of the Berryessa Snow Mountain National Monument

(from the Federal Register)
https://www.federalregister.gov/articles/2015/07/15/2015-17560/establishment-of-the-berryessa-snow-mountain-national-monument

Proclamation 9298 of July 10, 2015

A Proclamation

The Berryessa Snow Mountain area is the heart of northern California's wild Inner Coast Range. Once covered by ocean waters, it is a landscape shaped by geologic forces of staggering power overlain with bountiful but fragile biodiversity. Anchored in the north by Snow Mountain's remote forests and in the south by scenic Berryessa Mountain, this area stretches through unbroken wildlands and important wildlife corridors, a mosaic of native grasslands, picturesque oak woodlands, rare wetlands, and wild chaparral.

Home to the headwaters of the Eel River, and the Stony, Cache, and Putah creeks, Berryessa's waters are a crucial element of this landscape and a vital link to the water supply for millions of people. This dramatic and diverse landscape is a biological hotspot providing refuge for rare plant and animal species and showcasing the human history of north-central California.

Native Americans have inhabited these lands for at least the last 11,000 years. Many tribes, including the Yuki, Nomlaki, Patwin, Pomo, Huchnom, Wappo, and Lake Miwok, and Wintum all played a role in the history of this region, one of the most linguistically diverse in California.

The region's abundant natural resources helped to shape these distinct cultures. Early inhabitants subsisted upon protein-rich acorns in addition to seed and nut crops cultivated through traditional burning practices. Obsidian, chert, and basalt provided important source material for tool production, such as flaked tools and projectile points. The inhabitants also processed and produced both shell and magnesite beads, which they traded with other tribes.

Dense with cultural resources, the Berryessa Snow Mountain area contains a range of ancient settlements from mineral collection sites, and seasonal hunting and gathering camps in the high country, to major villages with subterranean, earth-covered round buildings in the lowlands. In addition to trade routes winding through the hills and mountains, the area is rich with sites that tell the story of early Native peoples: chert quarries where stone was gathered to make tools, task sites where tools were re-sharpened during hunting excursions, food sites where acorn and seeds were ground on large grindstones, and areas with pitted boulder petroglyphs where individuals illustrated their life experiences. The Cache Creek Archeological District, designated on the National Register of Historic Places, illustrates the area's archeological importance.

In the early 19th century, both Spanish and Mexican expeditions explored the region, as did fur trappers for the Hudson Bay Company. These explorers and trappers were often just brief visitors to this landscape, but their explorations and documentation opened the region to further European-American settlement by providing information about conditions, resources, and geography. This later settlement began during the 1840s gold rush. Farmingin the region was limited due to the difficult terrain and soils, while cattle and sheep ranching were much more profitable.

From the mid to late 1800s, many small sawmills operated within the forests of the area. The restored 1860s-era Nye homestead cabin, the historic Prather Mill, and remnants of associated railroad logging operations are tangible reminders of these historic uses. Around the turn of the 20th century, the mineral-laden waters and hot springs of the area attracted visitors to resorts and spas advertising their therapeutic benefits. Remains of the foundations of the mineral spring resorts at Bartlett Springs can be spotted by observant visitors today.

Native populations were displaced by the European-American settlement and development of the region in the early to mid-1800s. Many traditional hunting and gathering grounds were converted to grazing and logging and new diseases brought into the area spread to the Native people, greatly impacting the local Native populations and pushing them off of their homelands. Nevertheless, the region's landscape and resources retain deep cultural significance for modern Native communities, including roughly two dozen federally recognized tribes.

The Berryessa Snow Mountain area tells a dynamic geologic story. A relic of ancient times, scientists theorize that Snow Mountain formed as an underwater mountain during the Jurassic Period, 145-199 million years ago. Much of the region is prone to landslides due to weak and pervasively fractured rock, resulting in a diverse topography, including sag ponds and springs, with important values for wildlife and plants. The seismically active Bartlett Springs fault zone has remarkable features including hot springs and geologic outliers with marine invertebrate fossils dating to the Cretaceous Period and Cenozoic Era. The area has two important tension-crack caves, likely also created by landslides. These are classified as significant under the Federal Cave Resources Protection Act of 1988 and provide habitat for the Townsend's big-eared bat.

Rising from near sea-level in the south to over 7,000 feet in the mountainous north, and stretching across 100 miles and dozens of ecosystems, the area's species richness is among the highest in California. This internationally recognized biodiversity hotspot is located at the juncture between California's Klamath, North Coast, and Sacramento Vallejo ecoregions and provides vital habitat and migration corridors for diverse wildlife, including several endemic plant and animal species.

The Berryessa Snow Mountain area is notable for its significant concentration of serpentine soils arising from frequent seismic activity and influence from ancient oceans. Serpentine, California's State rock, is formed from the clashing, subduction, and rising of massive geologic forces, and can be found in significant quantity in the area. These soils lack the nutrients most plants need and often contain heavy metals toxic to many plants, resulting in plants that are unique and endemic to this region. Serpentine outcrops in the area have been the subject of a great deal of botanical, ecological, and evolutionary research, and hold promise for future scientific explorations. Many serpentine plants are listed as rare, sensitive, or threatened under Federal or State law. Examples are: the endemic bent-flowered fiddleneck and brittlescale, the Brewer's jewelflower, Purdy's fringed onion, musk brush, serpentine sunflower, bare monkeyflower, Indian Valley brodiaea, Red Mountain catchfly, and Snow Mountain buckwheat, along with numerous other herbs such as the Lake County stonecrop, coastal bluff morning glory, Cobb Mountain lupine, Contra Costa goldfields, and Napa western flax. There are also plant species that are near-endemics and almost entirely restricted to serpentine soils, such as MacNab cypress, leather oak, swamp larkspur, and Purdy's fritillary.

The Berryessa Snow Mountain area is replete with wild and unique landscapes and climatic micro-regions. These include Cedar Roughs, an important refuge for black bear and a 3,000-acre stand of endemic Sargent's cypresstrees. Cache Creek, a California Wild and Scenic River, provides an exceptional, intact riparian habitat and one of the largest wintering populations of bald eagles in the State. Remnants of the grassland prairies that once covered much of interior California still exist at Upper Cache Creek, where there are stands of native grasses with creeping wild rye and meadow barley, and some smaller relict patches of upland bunchgrass.

The 6,000-foot Goat Mountain is home to highly unusual plant assemblages that have created one of the most diverse butterfly regions in California. The Hale Ridge Research Natural Area hosts an important stand of knobcone pine. The ecological sky island of the 7,000-foot Snow Mountain serves as important habitat to a number of key plant and animal species.

The headwaters of the Bear Creek Watershed are a particularly excellent example of the area's serpentinite-based endemism and biodiversity with over 450 plant species, including a magnificent array of wildflowers, along with cypress, manzanita, and willow. Nearly half of California's 108 species of dragonfly and damselfly are found here, as well as 16 reptiles and amphibians, 6 rare insects, and 80 species of butterflies. This area has been an important focus of scientific studies on climate change, including studies of range shifts and isolated populations of species during Pleistocene changes in climate, and on post-fire succession.

The Berryessa Snow Mountain area's wide variety of elevations, many streams, ponds, and rivers as well as diverse plant communities provide excellent habitat for fish, wildlife, and amphibians. The streams and creeks in the Berryessa Snow Mountain area have served as centers for scientific research on hydrology and riparian ecosystems for decades. The riparian habitat linking the Sacramento River, Putah Creek, and Cache Creek provides a home for native birds such as the spotted sandpiper and the rare tricolored blackbird.

Waterways in the area harbor several native fish, including Pacific lamprey, western brook lamprey, rainbow trout, California roach, Sacramento pikeminnow, speckled dace, hardhead minnow, Clear Lake hitch, Sacramento sucker, and prickly and riffle sculpins. The area also provides historic habitat for coastal chinook salmon, Northern California steelhead, and California Central Valley steelhead.

Ponds and seeps throughout the area provide rare aquatic habitat for important plants like eelgrass pondweed, few-flowered navarretia, marsh checkerbloom, and Boggs Lake hedge-hyssop. This aquatic habitat is also home to amphibious species like the foothill yellow-legged frog, California red-legged frog, California newt, Pacific tree frog, western toad, and the northwestern pond turtle.

Numerous reptiles live in the Berryessa Snow Mountain area, including the St. Helena mountain king snake, western fence lizard, western skink, western whiptail, alligator lizard, gopher snake, common king snake, rubber boa, common garter snake, western terrestrial garter snake, western aquatic garter snake, and the northern Pacific rattlesnake.

Many large and small mammals co-exist in this diverse landscape, such as Tule elk, bobcats, mountain lions, black bears, mule deer, beaver, river otter, Pacific fishers, American badgers, Humboldt martens, and the San Joaquin pocket mouse. Most of the animal species in the area have special State or Federal status as sensitive, at-risk or threatened.

Raptors such as burrowing owls, prairie falcon, peregrine falcon, northern goshawk, and bald and golden eagles live and hunt throughout the upland areas. The Berryessa Snow Mountain area also serves as an important migratory corridor for neotropical birds and is home to a plethora of bat and insect species, including the threatened valley elderberry longhorn beetle and the vulnerable pallid bat, western sulphur butterfly, gray marble butterfly, Muir's hairstreak, and Lindsay's skipper.

The protection of the Berryessa Snow Mountain area will preserve its prehistoric and historic legacy and maintain its diverse array of scientific resources, ensuring that the prehistoric, historic, and scientific values remain for the benefit of all Americans. Today, the area is important for ranching and also provides outdoor recreation opportunities, including hunting, fishing, hiking, mountain biking, and horseback riding to a burgeoning population center.

WHEREAS, section 320301 of title 54, United States Code (known as the "Antiquities Act"), authorizes the President, in his discretion, to declare by public proclamation historic landmarks, historic and prehistoric structures, and other objects of historic or scientific interest that are situated upon the lands owned or controlled by the Federal Government to be national monuments, and to reserve as a part thereof parcels of land, the limits of which shall be confined to the smallest area compatible with the proper care and management of the objects to be protected;
WHEREAS, it is in the public interest to preserve the objects of scientific and historic interest on the lands of the Berryessa Snow Mountain area;

NOW, THEREFORE, I, BARACK OBAMA, President of the United States of America, by the authority vested in me by section 320301 of title 54, United States Code, hereby proclaim the objects identified above that are situated upon lands and interests in lands owned or controlled by the Federal Government to be the Berryessa Snow Mountain National Monument (monument) and, for the purpose of protecting those objects, reserve as part thereof all lands and interests in lands owned or controlled by the Federal Government within the boundaries described on the accompanying map, which is attached to and forms a part of this proclamation. These reserved Federal lands and interests in lands encompass approximately 330,780 acres. The boundaries described on the accompanying map are confined to the smallest area compatible with the proper care and management of the objects to be protected.

IN WITNESS WHEREOF, I have hereunto set my hand this tenth day of July, in the year of our Lord two thousand fifteen, and of the Independence of the United States of America the two hundred and fortieth.

Left to Right: Tom Tidwell, Chief, Forest Service; Cecilia Aguiar-Curry, Mayor of Winters; Congressman John Garamendi; Congressman Mike Thompson; Sally Jewell, U.S. Secretary of the Interior; President Obama; Assemblymember Bill Dodd; Congressman Jared Huffman; Judy Ahmann, Cattle Rancher, ANCW Cattlewoman of the Year and Tuleyome Board Member; Sara Husby, Executive Director of Tuleyome; Jose Gonzalez, Founder of Latino Outdoors; Christy Goldfuss, Managing Director at the White House Council on Environmental Quality.

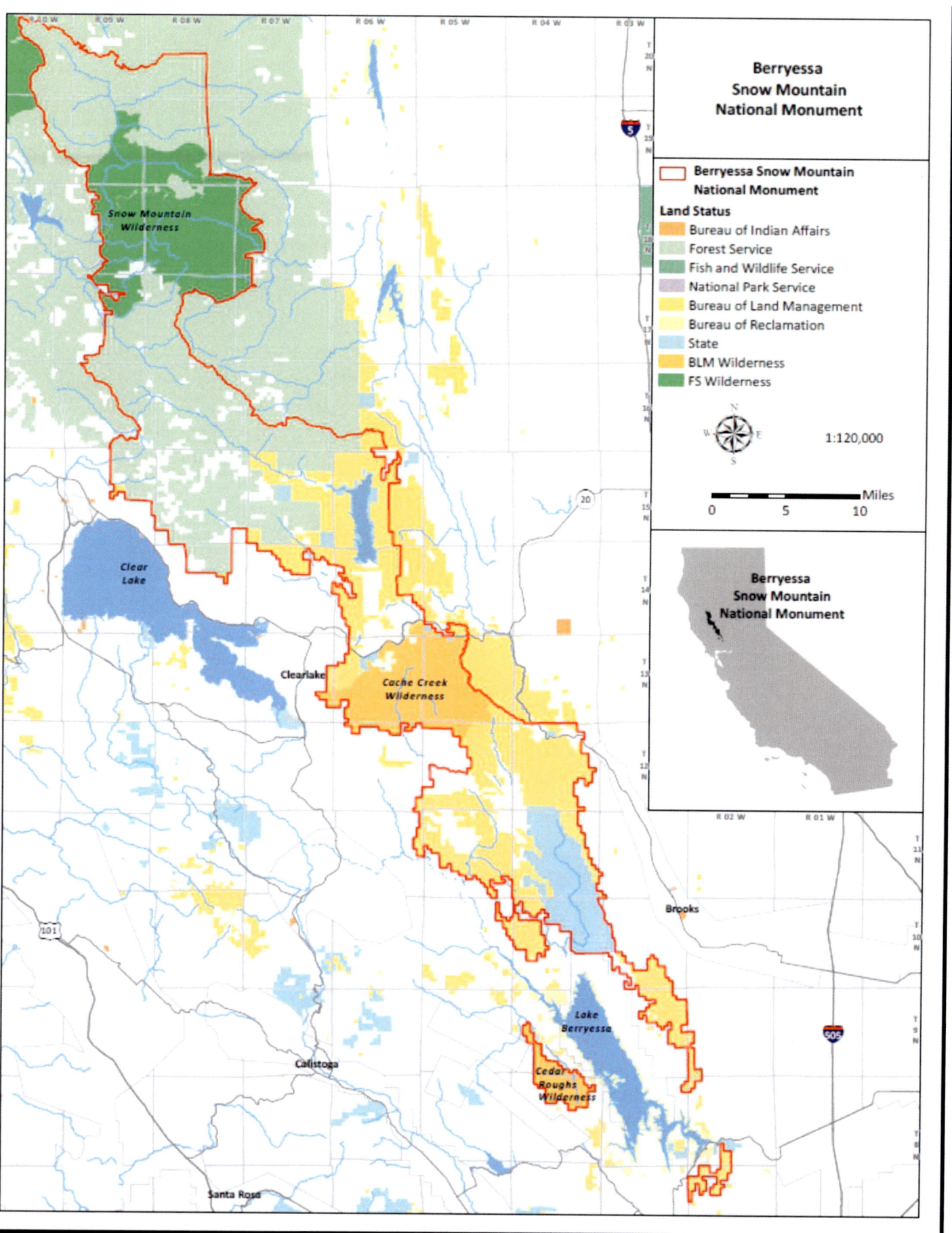

Federal and State of California Species Conservation Status Keys

The US Fish and Wildlife Service oversees the listing and protection of land animals and plants, along with fresh water fish on the federal level under the Endangered Species Act. In California, the California Department of Fish and Wildlife provides similar protections under the California Endangered Species Act. Species are only placed on the threatened or endangered lists after a petition is filed for protection and a careful review of the species -- including the urgency of its situation and whether other adequate protections exist elsewhere under the law -- has been conducted. Once a species qualifies it is listed as "threatened" or "endangered" and receives special protections under state and/or federal law. Protected animals cannot be "taken" (hunted, harmed or harassed, collected, shot, wounded, killed or captured). Listed plants are similarly protected if they are on state or federal land or are otherwise protected by state or federal action. The protection also extends to the animals' behavior and breeding habits, and to the habitat in which the protected species lives.

Federally Endangered Species — Listed by the US Federal Government as "Endangered", which is defined as a species that is in danger of extinction within the foreseeable future throughout all or a significant portion of its range.

Federally Threatened — Listed by the US Federal Government as "Threatened", which is defined as a species that is likely to become endangered within the foreseeable future throughout all or a significant portion of its range.

Federal Species of Special Concern — "Species of Special Concern" is an informal term. It is not defined in the federal Endangered Species Act. The term commonly refers to species that are declining or appear to be in need of conservation.

Endangered in California — Listed by the State of California as "Endangered", which is defined as a native species or subspecies of a bird, mammal, fish, amphibian, reptile or plant which is in serious danger of becoming extinct throughout all or a significant portion of its range due to one or more causes including loss of habitat, change of habitat, overexploitation, predation, competition or disease.

Threatened in California — Listed by the state of California as "Threatened", which is defined as a native species or subspecies of a bird, mammal, fish, amphibian, reptile, or plant that, although not presently threatened with extinction, is likely to become an endangered species in the foreseeable future in the absence of special protection and management efforts.

California Species of Special Concern — Listed by the California Department of Fish and Wildlife as a "Species of Special Concern", which is defined as a species, subspecies, or distinct population of an animal native to California that currently is experiencing, or formerly experienced, serious (noncyclical) population declines or range retractions (not reversed) that, if continued or resumed, could qualify it for State Threatened or Endangered status.

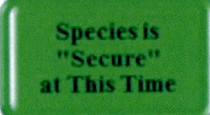

Species is "Secure" at This Time — Indicates that the species is doing well in the United States and California and/or is not currently on any "watch lists", or has not yet been evaluated for inclusion on a watch list because no one has filed a petition for protection under state or federal law.

NatureServe Ranking System

NatureServe is a non-profit conservation organization whose mission is to provide the scientific basis for effective conservation action. NatureServe and its network of natural heritage programs are the leading source for information about rare and endangered species and threatened ecosystems. NatureServe represents an international network of biological inventories known as natural heritage programs or conservation data centers operating in all 50 U.S. states, Canada, Latin America and the Caribbean. Together they not only collect and manage detailed local information on plants, animals, and ecosystems, but develop information products, data management tools, and conservation services to help meet local, national, and global conservation needs. The objective scientific information about species and ecosystems developed by NatureServe is used by all sectors of society, conservation groups, government agencies, corporations, academia, and the public to make informed decisions about managing our natural resources. For more information, visit www.natureserve.org.

⇒ **Listed by NatureServe as Secure** – a species that is common, widespread, and abundant.
⇒ **Listed by NatureServe as Apparently Secure** – a species that is uncommon but not rare; there is some cause for long-term concern due to declines or other factors.
⇒ **Listed by NatureServe Vulnerable** – a species at moderate risk of extinction or elimination due to a restricted range, relatively few populations, recent and widespread declines, or other factors.
⇒ **Listed by NatureServe as Imperiled** – a species at high risk of extinction or elimination due to very restricted range, very few populations, steep declines, or other factors.
⇒ **Listed by NatureServe as Critically Imperiled** – a species at very high risk of extinction due to extreme rarity (often 5 or fewer populations), very steep declines, or other factors.

California Native Plant Society Plant Ranking System

The California Native Plant Society (CNPS) Originally formed in 1965, and is a statewide non-profit organization of amateurs and professionals with a common interest in California's native plants. The mission of the California Native Plant Society is to increase understanding and appreciation of California's native plants and to conserve them and their natural habitats through education, science, advocacy, horticulture and land stewardship. The Program, since its inception in 1968, has developed a reputation for scientific accuracy and integrity. The Program's data are widely accepted as the standard for information on the rarity and endangerment status of the California flora. For more information, visit www.cnps.org.

⇒ **List 1B – Plants that are Rare, Threatened, or Endangered in California and elsewhere.** The plants of List 1B are rare throughout their range with the majority of them endemic to California. Most of the plants of List 1B have declined significantly over the last century. List 1B plants constitute the majority of the plants in CNPS' Inventory with more than 1,000 plants assigned to this category of rarity. All of the plants constituting List 1B meet the definitions of Sec. 1901, Chapter 10 (Native Plant Protection Act) or Secs. 2062 and 2067 (California Endangered Species Act) of the California Department of Fish and Game Code, and are eligible for state listing.
⇒ **List 2 – Plants Rare, Threatened, or Endangered in California, But More Common Elsewhere.** Except for being common beyond the boundaries of California, the plants of List 2 would have appeared on List 1B. With List 2, we recognize the importance of protecting the geographic range of widespread species. In this way we protect the diversity of our own state's flora and help maintain evolutionary process and genetic diversity within species. All of the plants constituting List 2 meet the definitions of Sec. 1901, Chapter 10 (Native Plant Protection Act) or Secs. 2062 and 2067 (California Endangered Species Act) of the California Department of Fish and Game Code, and are eligible for state listing.
⇒ **List 4 – Plants of Limited Distribution—A Watch List.** The plants in this category are of limited distribution or infrequent throughout a broader area in California, and their vulnerability or susceptibility to threat appears relatively low at this time.

Threat Ranks

⇒ **0.1 – Seriously threatened in California** (high degree/immediacy of threat)
⇒ **0.2 – Fairly threatened in California** (moderate degree/immediacy of threat)
⇒ **0.3 – Not very threatened in California** (low degree/immediacy of threats or no current threats known)

Baby Coyote photos by Roger Jones, Certified Wildlife Biologist and Sr. Natural Resource Specialist at the SRWTP Bufferlands

FAUNA

- Birds
- Insects
  - Common Wasp Galls
- Mammals
- Reptiles, Fish, Amphibians

Acorn Woodpecker (*Melanerpes formicivorus*)

Acorn Woodpecker on one of its "granary" trees. Photo by Mary K. Hanson.

Species is "Secure" at This Time

Primary Habitat: This woodpecker prefers valley and foothill oak woodlands, oak-pine woodlands, and oak savannas. Less frequently, they also occupy mixed-evergreen forests, chaparral and savanna grasslands. They may also be common in residential areas where oaks are present.

These birds can often be found around their "granary" trees: dead trees stocked full of acorns placed there by the woodpeckers.

Primary Threat(s): Although this species is not considered threatened, populations can be gravely affected by starvation due to habitat loss and degradation of habitat or overgrazing of local oak trees, hybridization of native oak trees with exotic oak trees, destruction of oak forests for firewood, and commercial or private development of oak forest areas.

American Peregrine Falcon, "Duck Falcon" (*Falco peregrinus anatum*)

Endangered in California

Primary Habitat: This falcon is found on Blue Ridge. Nesting sites are typically found on the west side of the ridge where the steep cliffs are. *Falco peregrinius anatum* is one of 19 subspecies of Peregrine Falcon, and is found only in the United States and parts of Canada.

It used to be all over the country, but now the eastern populations are extinct.

This falcon has dark blue-gray wings, a dark head and a barred white breast. Best known for its speed, this raptor can dive at up to 200 miles per hour in one of its death-drops onto prey. Females are larger than the males. Falcons mate for life and return to the same nesting sites year after year. Also called "Duck Falcons", this subspecies lives primarily on other birds, including many species of waterfowl.

Peregrine Hawk photos by Doug Donaldson.

Primary Threat(s): Expanding development, wind energy development, and chlorinated hydrocarbon pesticides.

Bald Eagle (*Haliaeetus leucocephalus*)

Primary Habitat: Found on wetland and lake margins, this eagle nests and winters near rivers, creeks and other water regions where it roosts communally.

Some of the best viewing in the region is along Cache Creek and at the Sacramento National Wildlife Preserve on the border of Colusa and Glenn Counties.

The Berryessa Snow Mountain region is home to the second largest population of wintering Bald Eagles in the state.

Primary Threat(s): Power line construction, residential development, and wind energy development, lead in the environment.

The Bald Eagle is projected to have only 26 % of its current summer range remaining by 2080, according to Audubon's climate model. However, it could potentially recover 73 % of its summer range if new areas open up by a shifting climate.

Once listed on the Endangered Species list, the Bald Eagle was removed from the list once its numbers recovered sufficiently. Bald Eagles are, however, still protected under the Migratory Bird Treaty Act and the Bald and Golden Act. It is illegal to trap or kill Bald Eagles.

Photo by Mary K. Hanson

Bank Swallow, "Sand Martin" (*Riparia riparia*)

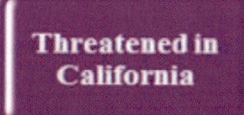
Threatened in California

Primary Habitat: A colonial nester, Bank Swallows nest only in vertical, collapsing sandy riverbanks, in alluvial soils along rivers, streams and lakes, and are regionally found near riparian and other lowland habitats, such as those along the banks of Cache Creek. They are small birds with slender bodies and long wings. The most distinctive marking is a band across the chest which can extend to the middle of the belly. The swallows eat insects, usually "on the fly", over water sources. Audubon's climate model forecasts substantial movement northward and slight range expansion for the species, but only 22% of the current summer range remains suitable.

Primary Threat(s): Bank Swallows are threatened by habitat destruction due to agriculture, aggregate mining, major dams, and other activities that change river hydrology, removing sandy riverside deposits. *The presence of bank swallows in a river basin is a sign of riparian health and hydrological integrity.*

Public Domain Photo from Creative Commons courtesy of Shawn McCready.

Black-Crowned Night Heron *(Nycticorax nycticorax)*

Photo by Sylvia Wright.

Threatened in California

Primary Habitat: Forests, scrub and shrub areas, marshes and ponds; especially along the edges of ponds and creeks. Some of the best viewing is at Conaway Ranch, Cache Creek, the Yolo Basin, along the American River (especially near the Nimbus Fish Hatchery) and the Sacramento National Wildlife Preserve.

Primary Threat(s): Habitat loss, pesticides and herbicides, water pollution, climate change. Audubon's climate model forecasts that both summer and winter ranges will spread northward, but that only 12% of the North American summer range will remain stable.

Cooper's Hawk *(Accipiter cooperii)*

Cooper's Hawk photo by Roger Jones.

Listed by NatureServe Vulnerable in California – a species at moderate risk of extinction or elimination due to a restricted range, relatively few populations, recent and widespread declines, or other factors.

Primary Habitat: This hawk prefers open, interrupted, or riparian woodlands. Population numbers have stabilized or are increasing in some parts of its range, but the species has not fully recovered from its drastic decline from 1940 to 1970 throughout much of the eastern part of the range. The hawks' decline was caused in part by DDT poisoning (which caused egg shell thinning), and in part because the hawks, which often prey on chickens, were viewed as pest animals and were persecuted by farmers almost to the point of extinction. Reasons for its current lack of recovery are unknown.

These hawks can be seen throughout Yolo and Sacramento County, especially around Conaway Ranch and the Sacramento Regional County Sanitation District Bufferlands.

Primary Threat(s): Habitat loss due to logging, agriculture, and other development. It is also potentially threatened by the use of "organochlorine" biocides; lead poisoning.

Burrowing Owl *(Athene cunicularia)*

Photos by Wendy E. Miller. Some rights reserved.

California Species of Special Concern

Primary Habitat: **Native** to California, Burrowing Owls are found in open, dry, annual or perennial grasslands, and scrublands characterized by low growing vegetation. Although the owls can dig their own burrows, they usually let other animal species do that for them and take over the abandoned homes of ground squirrels, skunks and rodents. They often line the burrow with manure (to attract dung beetles which they then eat).

There are several populations in and around Davis, California including the greenbelt around the Wildhorse Golf Club and at Yolo County Grasslands Regional Park. They prefer landscapes that are dry, without trees, have short grass and have an abundance of other ground-dwelling animals.

Burrowing Owls catch insects, scorpions, small mammals and reptiles with their feet, often by running along the ground and pouncing on their prey.

Primary Threat(s): Loss of burrows due to rodent-control activities and expanding development; insecticides which kill their prey species.

For more information see the Burrowing Qwls Preservation Society website at: burrowingowlpreservation.org/.

Double-Crested Cormorant *(Phalacrocorax auritus)*

Photo by Ron Dudley.

Primary Habitat: Strictly a North American species, this bird prefers estuaries, and inland freshwater areas including those near ponds, lakes and rivers as its habitat. Up to several hundred pairs nest at lakes and reservoirs throughout the northern and central California counties of Siskiyou, Modoc, Lassen, Lake, Yolo, and Sacramento. Some large flocks and individuals can be found around the Nimbus Fish Hatchery, the Yolo Bypass Wildlife Area, along Putah Creek and Lake Solano (where the birds sometimes complete with fishermen for fish), and even some urban ponds (like those in William Land Park in Sacramento). They can often be seen standing on rocks, tree limbs, outcroppings or high tension lines with their wings outstretched, drying themselves in the sun.

These Cormorants are dark, heavy-bodied birds with snake-like necks. Surprisingly, their eyes are a brilliant aquamarine-blue, set off by the yellow-orange skin on the face. The inside of their mouths is also bright blue. The "double-crest" on the head of these Cormorants is only visible during mating season.

Primary Threat(s): loss of habitat, water pollution, and human interference. While the impact of direct human harassment and disturbance on Double-Crested Cormorant populations in the U.S. has declined substantially since they were protected in 1972 under the Migratory Bird Treaty Act, nesting cormorants remain sensitive to human disturbance, particularly during the early incubation and early nestling-rearing stages (Ellison and Cleary 1978, Hatch and Weseloh 1999). Audubon's climate model for this species predicts a significant shift in summer climate space by 2080—only 21% of the core area remains stable.

Egret, Cattle Egret *(Bubulcus ibis)*

Public Domain Photo from http://commons.wikimedia.org/

Species is "Secure" at This Time

Primary Habitat: The Cattle Egret is well-adapted to a variety of habitats (both aquatic and terrestrial). Cattle Egrets may be found throughout the state in savanna/grasslands, forests, scrub forests, wetlands, rice paddies, farmland and pastures (with nesting sites nearby). Unlike other egrets, the Cattle Egret typically feeds in dry fields, often following livestock or other animals that flush insects up as they graze. Although insects are the mainstay of their diet, these egrets also eat snakes, worms, birds' eggs and nestlings, and fish. Some ranchers rely on Cattle Egrets for fly control more than they do pesticides. Locally, these birds can often be seen throughout the Yolo Bypass area and Conaway Ranch.

Cattle Egrets are about 20 inches tall (long) with a yellow bill and yellow-gray legs. They are usually white, but in the breeding season, the males develop buff-colored feathers on the back, chest and crown.

Primary Threat(s): Persecution by humans who see the birds as a nuisance; pesticide poisoning; degradation and destruction of nesting sites; wetland drainage; hydroelectric power plants near breeding areas.

Egret, Great Egret *(Ardea alba)*

Primary Habitat: Unlike the Cattle Egret, the Great Egret depends on aquatic landscapes such as marshes and wetlands for its survival. It can also be seen foraging in flooded pastureland, rice paddies, and along drainage ditches, creeks, and ponds. They feed alone for crawfish, frogs, snakes, fish, and snails, and occasionally small mammals like mice.

Species is "Secure" at This Time

Photo by Mary K. Hanson

Easily distinguished from the Cattle Egret by its large size, the Great Egret stands over 3 feet tall and has a wingspan of over 5 feet. Its bill is yellow and its legs are black. Plumage is white regardless of season, but in the breeding season the males develop extra-long lacy plumes that curl down over the tail, and a patch of skin on the face turns brilliant green.

Primary Threat(s): loss of habitat due to draining of wetlands; water pollution; insecticide and pesticide poisoning and contaminated run-off from sewers. Although their numbers in the US are healthy, the Great Egrets were almost wiped out in the late 1800's and early 1900's simply for the use of their plumes in ladies hats. The National Audubon Society was initially formed to protect these birds from predation and exploitation by humans, and now the Great Egret is the symbol of that organization.

Egret, Snowy Egret *(Egretta thula)*

Photo by Mary K. Hanson

Primary Habitat: Like the Great Egret, Snowy Egrets are found in marshes and wetlands, alongside rivers, streams and creeks, in flooded pastures and rice paddies, and near ponds. Unlike the Great Egrets (which are solitary foragers), Snowy Egrets eat in groups, dining primarily on fish, crustaceans, small reptiles and frogs. They are often seen along the Sacramento and American Rivers and their tributaries.

The Snowy Egret, at about 2 feet tall, is in between the Cattle Egret and Great Egret in size. It's distinguished by its black beak, black legs and bright yellow feet. Plumage is always white, regardless of season, but in mating season a patch of skin on the face blushes red and they grow extra-long curving plumes on the back. Males select breeding sites, but both the male and female build the nest. Snowy Egrets breed in large colonies.

Species is "Secure" at This Time

Primary Threat(s): loss of habitat due to draining of wetlands; water pollution; insecticide and pesticide poisoning and contaminated run-off from sewers. Like other egrets, Snowy Egrets were once hunted and killed for their mating plumage. This practice was outlawed in the early 1900's.

Ferruginous Hawk *(Buteo regalis)*

California Species of Special Concern

Primary Habitat: California range is "south from the Oregon line, east of the humid coast belt, to Mexican line chiefly west of Colorado desert" (Ca. Dept. of Fish & Wildlife); grasslands, and shrub-steppe habitat. **Winters extensively in California**.

Populations can often be found at the Hunt-Wesson Hawk and Owl Preserve, a cooperative venture between the Yolo Audubon Society (YAS) and the Hunt-Wesson Company located just west of the Yolo County Landfill on Road 28H. Occasionally Ferruginous Hawks can be found in farmland throughout Yolo county. According to the Central Valley Bird Club: *"Roads 27, 29, 29A, 31, 95, 98, 99, and 102 all offer rural birding opportunities. However, Roads 31, 98, and 102 carry fairly heavy traffic, so the other roads are quieter, with better opportunities to see birds. Appropriate places to pull off and stop safely are scarce, so great care is needed when stopping."*

In Sacramento County the birds are sometimes found near the Cosumnes River Preserve, especially along Desmond and Bruceville Roads.

Primary Threat(s): human-induced disturbances (especially in breeding areas); loss of prey animals; strychnine poisoning (from eating poisoned ground squirrels).

Audubon's climate model now projects a significant shift (only 6% remaining stable) and reduction (by 84%) of summer climate space for this species.

Photo by Sylvia Wright.

Golden Eagle *(Aquila chrysaetos)*

Listed by NatureServe Vulnerable in California – a species at moderate risk of extinction or elimination due to a restricted range, relatively few populations, recent and widespread declines, or other factors.

Primary Habitat: The Golden Eagle is found in rolling foothills, mountain areas, and sage/juniper flats, grasslands and oak woodlands. These birds may be found wintering throughout the Berryessa Snow Mountain region.

Golden Eagles are sometimes confused with immature Bald Eagles, but a quick way to tell the two apart is to look at the feathering on the legs. The lower legs of the Golden Eagles are covered with feathers down to their toes; the lower legs of Bald Eagles are bare.

Primary Threat(s): Recreation, habitat destruction, loss of foraging areas, lead in the environment and pesticide poisoning. Wind energy development has been a recent culprit in the deaths of Golden Eagles.

By 2080, Golden Eagles are projected to lose 41% of their breeding range and 16% of their non-breeding range, according to Audubon's climate model. Its abundance in California is unknown but its numbers seem to be in decline across it range (CA Dept. of Fish and Wildlife).

Golden Eagle. Photo by Ron Dudley.

Great Blue Heron *(Ardea herodias)*

Primary Habitat: Mature forests near foraging sites; marshlands and riparian areas are preferred. In fall and early winter, adult and juvenile herons often prey on small mammals in fallow, freshly plowed, or mowed fields and in grasslands. Herons also feed in ditches, old fields, marshes, and wetlands just following their dispersal from breeding areas.

California Species of Special Concern

In Yolo County they can often be seen foraging in the local rice fields and the Yolo Basin. They are common visitors to Putah Creek, Lake Berryessa, and other waterways. They also congregate near local fish hatcheries, and there is a large breeding colony (over 100 nests) in the Bufferlands area in Sacramento County.

The largest herons in North America, these herons are slate-grey overall with a black stripe over the eye. They have special bib feathers on the chest called "powder down" which they use to remove fish slime and other matter from their feathers as they preen. The oldest banded Great Blue Heron lived to be 24 years old.

Primary Threat(s): Loss of habitat, development, and human disturbance of nesting sites are the chief threats to these large birds.

Photo by Mary K. Hanson

Great Horned Owl *(Bubo virginianus)*

Species is "Secure" at This Time

Great Horned Owl. Photo by Roger Jones.

Primary Habitat: coniferous and deciduous forests, oak woodlands, orchards, second growth forests, marshes, riverine forests, partially wooded slopes, brushy hillsides, farm woodlots, and large city parks. Nesting pairs can be found in the Cache Creek Wilderness Preserve, the American RiverParkway, the Bufferlands in Sacramento County, the Yolo Bypass Wildlife Area, and in the Davis Arboretum in Yolo County, among other places. These birds typically nest in cottonwood, oak, juniper and pine trees.

A major predator, a Great Horned Owl can take down prey animals larger than itself.

Females are larger than males, but the males have a larger voice box, so their hooting calls have a deep resonant sound.

Primary Threat(s): Although currently stable, a decline in prey-animals, human disturbance, drought, climate change and other factors may impact future populations.

Green Heron *(Butorides virescens)*

Species is "Secure" at This Time

Primary Habitat: Inland wetlands, swamps and marshes, lakes, ponds and rivers where trees and shrubs can provide secluded nesting sites. Some nest in dry woods, riparian habitat, orchards and urban parks (such as William Land Park in Sacramento). Populations have also been found around the Nimbus Fish Hatchery, Lake Solano, and the Yolo Bypass Wildlife Area. They are also frequent visitors to local fish hatcheries.

About the size of a crow, this is the smallest heron in the state. It looks brown from a distance, but closer inspection will reveal its dark green iridescent feathers. The feathers on the top of the head can be raised when the bird is threatened or distressed. The Green Heron also a "tool using" bird that will use twigs, feathers, dead bugs and other lures to attract fish. It will drop the lure on the surface of the water, and then grab the fish that approaches it. "Tuleyome Tales" author Mary K. Hanson once noted that she watched a Green Heron at an urban pond use a "Cheeto" as its lure, and on another occasion got photos of a Green Heron fishing with a dead bee.

This heron's diet consists mainly of small fish, like minnows, but they will also eat such things as insects, spiders, snails, and small reptiles.

Primary Threat(s): habitat loss through the draining or development of wetlands; water pollution.

Green Heron. Photo by Mary K. Hanson.

Mountain Bluebird *(Sialia currucoides)*

Public Domain Photo from http://www.public-domain-image.com/

Primary Habitat: Wide-open spaces at middle– or upper elevations; prairies, sagebrush steppes, pastures and even alpine areas. They prefer areas with a mix of short grasses, shrubs and trees, but also like meadows, alpine hillsides, and recently burned or clear-cut areas. They also adapt to human-altered habitats and sometimes nest in manmade bluebird boxes.

Primary Threat(s): Loss of habitat; competition for nesting cavities with other birds; climate change. Habitat lost to agriculture or deforestation has been replaced in some regions where man-made nesting boxes are made readily available to the birds.

According to Audubon's climate-change report this species will suffer a "potentially severe loss of current summer range by 2080; may be most acute at high elevations, where meadows are widely expected to suffer from climate change."

Species is "Secure" at This Time

Northern Flicker, "Western Flicker" *(Colaptes auratus)*

Male Flicker. Photo by Mary K. Hanson

Species is "Secure" at This Time

Primary Habitat: Deciduous, mixed and coniferous woodlands, forest edge and riparian woodlands, wetland areas (with standing trees), meadows, parks and farmland (with large nearby trees). Locally, these birds can be found throughout the region, along the American and Sacramento Rivers, at the Cache Creek Nature Preserve, the American River Bend Park, the Putah Creek Wildlife Area, and the Sacramento National Wildlife Preserve, among many other places.

A large woodpecker, this one is quite striking in coloration. When it's in flight you can see a flash of white tufted feathers right above the tail. The Flickers in the West are called "red shafted" which differentiates them from their Eastern "yellow shafted" cousins. Females are less brightly colored than males.

Flickers usually forage on the ground for ants, beetle larvae and grasshoppers, but also eat fruits, berries and seeds in the winter months.

Primary Threat(s): Loss of habitat (especially where old scag trees are pulled down), competition with invasive European Starlings, predation, use of pesticides and herbicides on lawns and in agriculture.

Northern Goshawk *(Accipiter gentilis)*

Primary Habitat: The Northern Gosshawk is found within and near deciduous and coniferous forests. They prefer dense forests with large trees and canopy covers that are high, but can occupy a variety of structural conditions. Their core breeding range in most of the northern Coast Ranges and populations are found in Mendocino County.

California Species of Special Concern

Powerful predators, they use speed and ambush to capture prey.

Primary Threat(s): Habitat destruction due to logging and other forest management activities, and wind energy development. In California they also compete with other raptors for nesting sites.

There have been two petitions to have the Goshawk listed as "Endangered" but they were turned down in part due to pressure from the timber industry. A third petition is now before the courts and a decision is pending as of the writing of this book.

Public Domain Photo from http://www.public-domain-image.com/

Prairie Falcon *(Falco mexicanus)*

Listed by NatureServe Vulnerable in California – a species at moderate risk of extinction or elimination due to a restricted range, relatively few populations, recent and widespread declines, or other factors.

Primary Habitat: Prairie Falcons are found in dry, open grassland terrain (with nesting sites nearby) along cliff sites and prairies. They can forage far afield. Ground squirrels are their major food source, and they help to keep populations in check, but they will also eat European Starlings, Cliff Swallows and other birds, as well as retiles and snakes. This is the bird most often used in "falconry". (For more information about falconry opportunities in the region see the West Coast Falconry website at: http://westcoast-falconry.com/)

According to a Yolo Natural Heritage Program report, Prairie Falcons have been found breeding in the Blue Ridge area, and *"are uncommonly, but regularly observed in the Cache Creek watershed year round."*

A large falcon it is easily recognized by the dark "mustache" marks on its face and dark "arm pits".

Primary Threat(s): Grazing, wind energy development, and other development that cause breeding habitat loss.

Photo by Sylvia Wright.

Red-Shouldered Hawk (Buteo lineatus)

Species is "Secure" at This Time

Primary Habitat: Open grassland habitats; prefer large areas with mixed deciduous/conifer woodlands, riparian woodlands, oak woodlands and in eucalyptus groves. They will also frequent wetland areas where there are trees nearby. Females of the species are generally larger than the males. The tail of the both immature and mature red-shouldered hawks is dark brown with white bands which helps to distinguish it from the Red-Tailed Hawk.

Red-Shouldered Hawk. Photo by Mary K. Hanson.

These hawks can be found throughout the region including at the American River Bend Park, the Cache Creek Nature Preserve, Putah Creek, Lake Solano, the Cosumnes River Preserve and the Yolo Bypass Wildlife Area. They can often be found sitting on the fence posts along the roadways in the region.

Primary Threat(s): Habitat loss, loss of prey animals, pesticides, lead poisoning, being hit by cars where nesting/foraging areas are adjacent to highways, loss of nesting habitat.

Red-Tailed Hawk (Buteo jamaicensis)

Red-Tailed Hawk. Photo by Ron Dudley.

Primary Habitat: covers a wide range of habitats and altitudes including grasslands, forests (except for sub-alpine and alpine forests), open land areas, agricultural fields and urban areas. The most common hawk in North America, the Red-Tailed Hawk can be seen throughout the Berryessa Snow Mountain region.

Species is "Secure" at This Time

Along with the standard coloration, there are dark-morph Red-Tails that are a rich chocolate brown overall, and rufous-morph Ref-Tails with a reddish-brown chest and dark belly. According to a *Dixon Patch* article by Ken Ealy, *"The red-tailed hawk mates for life, as do most other raptors. The famous red tail is acquired after the first two years of life, so the young hawks will have a brown tail with prominent horizontal stripes (barring)."* According to the All About Birds website, whenever a hawk or eagle (regardless of species) appears in a movie or television show, it's usually the Red-Tail Hawk's distinctive shrill raspy scream that is used for sound effect purposes.

Primary Threat(s): Because this bird is found throughout the state in a variety of different landscapes, its numbers have increased significantly. Primary threats include poisoning of food sources (with pesticides or lead).

Red-Winged Blackbird *(Agelaius phoeniceus)*

California Species of Special Concern

Primary Habitat: These birds breed in wet places like fresh water marshes and rice paddies. They may also be found in sedge meadows, alfalfa fields, grasslands, seed lots and pastures. Locally, large colonies can be found in the Yolo Basin, Conaway Ranch, the Cosumnes River Preserve and the Sacramento National Wildlife Refuge.

Adult males of this species are black with bright red epaulets trimmed with yellow. There is another species with red epaulets timed in white called a "Tri-Colored Blackbird". Females are brown and look like large sparrows.

Primary Threat(s): Red-winged Blackbird populations have declined by over 30% throughout most of their range since 1966, according to the North American Breeding Bird Survey. Threats include degradation and loss of breeding habitat from residential development, a lowered water table, exotic invasive plant species, and predation by humans who may see the birds as a threat to agricultural fields.

Red-Winged Blackbird. Photo by Roger Jones.

Rough-Legged Hawk, "Rough-Legged Buzzard" *(Buteo lagopus)*

Primary Habitat: During the winter these birds prefer marshes, prairies and agricultural areas where rodent populations are dense; otherwise, they can be found in areas where there is a lot of unforested open-ground. Some Rough-Legs nest on cliff sides, others nest in trees or on the ground. In Yolo County you may spot these birds along County Roads 16, 17, 101 and 102.

Species is "Secure" at This Time

Their legs are feathered down to the toes -- which gives rise to their name "Rough-Legged". The females' markings differ from the males, and there are light- and dark-morph color patterns. When perching, the bird's wingtips reach back to the tail tip. The tail is white at the base regardless of color morph. Commonly these hawks have a pale streaked chest and dark belly.

Primary Threat(s): because Rough-Leg populations can vary greatly depending on prey density, it's difficult to get an overall accurate account of their numbers. The greatest threats are a loss of prey animals (small mammals), and competition for nesting sites with other large birds.

Photo by Sylvia Wright.

Scrub Jay, California Scrub Jay *(Aphelocoma californica)*

California Scrub Jay. Photo by Ron Dudley.

Primary Habitat: Oak woodlands, riparian areas, scrubby chapparal, and pinyon pine/juniper forests. They will also nest and forage in urban and rural area populated by humans where there are oak trees readily available to the birds. These jays can be found in all of the counties that comprise the Berryessa Snow Mountain region.

They have a blue head with white eyebrows, a long blue tail, white breast and gray back.

Scrub Jays were included in a study done by the University of California in Davis in 2011 during it was found that the birds respond with cacophonous cries and other "funeral" vocalizations when faced with a dead Scrub Jay. They recognize their own species, and they recognize their own dead.

Primary Threat(s): Loss of habitat.

Species is "Secure" at This Time

Short-Eared Owl *(Asio flammeus)*

California Species of Special Concern

Primary Habitat: Fresh-water marshlands, irrigated alfalfa or grain fields, open country, ungrazed grasslands and old pastures. Tule marsh or tall grasslands can support nesting pairs. Locally there are very small resident populations in Sacramento, Butte, Sutter, and Yolo County. Other populations are migratory and are dependent upon an abundance of prey animals especially voles. Productive habitat for resident owls in California is now almost entirely limited to wildlife refuges and management areas.

These owls live on small mammals and sometimes smaller birds. They locate prey by sound (not by sight) -- their facial disks funnel sound to their ears -- while they fly low over the ground. Short-Eared Owls build their nests on the ground in shallow dug outs

Primary Threat(s): Habitat loss and degradation, aggravated to an unknown extent by overgrazing, invasive exotic weeds, water management, and disease. In addition, Short-Eared Owls are also susceptible to collisions with automobiles where paved roads cross wetland or grassland habitats. The 2014 State of the Birds Report listed them as a "Common Bird in Steep Decline."

Short-Eared Owl along Road 35, Yolo County. Photo by Sylvia Wright.

Spotted Towhee, Western Spotted Towhee *(Pipilo maculatus)*

Species is "Secure" at This Time

Primary Habitat: These birds like heavy brush areas, dry thickets, forest edges, chaparral... and even suburban areas where there is dense shrub cover and plenty of leaf-litter through which to forage for insects, spiders, and the occasional small reptile. They also eat acorns, berries and seeds, grains and cherries. Shy, reclusive birds they tend to hop with both feet (often backwards) as they search for food. They nest near or at ground-level. Males have a black head and throat, black wings with white spots, and russet-colored flanks. Females are similarly patterned but have a slimmer build. Both genders have bright red eyes. These birds can be found throughout the Berryessa Snow Mountain region.

Male Spotted Towhee. Photo by Mary K. Hanson

Male towhees have been recorded spending 70% to 90% of their mornings singing. Almost as soon as they attract a mate, their attention shifts to other things, and they spend only about 5% of their time singing. These birds have a wide range of vocalizations, including a long, buzzy "*cheweeeee!*"

Primary Threat(s): Destruction of habitat (although these bird do often adapt well in developed areas where there are brushes hedges and leaf-litter available).

Steller's Jay *(Cyanocitta stelleri)*

Primary Habitat: In California, it is a common to uncommon resident in coniferous or dense hardwood habitats throughout the state. Trees, especially large, mature trees and shrubs provide cover for Steller's Jays. They generally prefer conifers but are frequently found in hardwood habitats. Populations have been found around Lake Solano.

Species is "Secure" at This Time

Distinguishing characteristics are their pointed black bill and their tall black crest. Their diet generally consists of acorns, pine seeds, and nuts, but they are also notorious for scavenging at picnic sites within their range. Like other jays, Steller's Jays are noisy, inquisitive and intelligent.

There are approximately 16 subspecies of the Steller Jay in Northern and Central America. The dark blue Pacific species has thin blue stripes up the forehead between the eyes.

Primary Threat(s): Steller's Jay populations remained stable between 1966 and 2010, according to the North American Breeding Bird Survey. Climate change may eventually effect where this bird winters.

Public Domain Photo from http://commons.wikimedia.org/

Swainson's Hawk *(Buteo swainsoni)*

LEFT: Photo by Ron Dudley. Photo above is public domain through Wikimedia Commons

Threatened in California

Primary Habitat: With the loss of much of its open grasslands habitat, this hawk it has become increasingly dependent on agriculture as native communities are converted to agricultural lands. They nest in riparian regions adjacent to fields or pastures, or in tall trees adjacent to foraging habitat. In Yolo County, they can be found almost anywhere along the valley floor hunting for prey. Nesting areas include the cities of Davis and Woodland. The largest breeding population in the state is located in the midsection of the Central Valley in the area between Sacramento and Modesto. In 2015 they were frequently sighted along I5.

They feed their chicks rodents, rabbits and snakes, but outside of the breeding season, the adults usually eat a lot of insects (especially dragonflies and grasshoppers) which they chase across the ground. Their coloring can be quite variable -- with light-, dark-, and intermediate-morphs -- but most males have gray heads while the females have brown heads. Very dark individuals can also be found: from deep reddish brown to nearly black. These birds are social animals. When it's not breeding season, they can often be found in groups, sometimes flying in kettles (soaring in circles up into the sky) like Turkey Vultures.

The ICUN Red List does not list this hawk as "threatened" because it's populations stable or growing throughout the world. However, it does note that *"certain regions have seen declines, particularly in California where only an estimated 10% of the original population remains."* Historically, the Swainson's Hawk population was around 17,000 pairs. Surveys done for the Department of Fish and Wildlife in the Central Valley area, however, reported that only about 430 mating pairs remained in 1988. Surveys since that time have shown the hawk's population density improving (up to 2080 pairs in 2005 statewide), but it is still nowhere near its historic numbers. The cause of the decline is not fully understood, although loss of habitat seems to be the greatest issue. The DFW also warns that the increase in population between 1988 and 2005 should not be viewed as a "trend" because there isn't enough data to support that contention. Some of the data may be skewed, they note, because of the renewed interest in the Swainson's Hawk which causes more people to simply be more aware of the birds and their numbers.

For more information about these birds see the Friends of Swainson's Hawk website at: www.swainsonshawk.org.

Primary Threat(s): Loss of habitat, wind turbines, climate change, pesticide poisoning and electrocution.

Tricolored Blackbird *(Agelaius tricolor)*

Dr. Bob Meese prepares to release a banded Tricolored Blackbird at Conaway Ranch in Yolo County, CA. Photo by Sylvia Wright.

Federal Species of Special Concern

Endangered in California

Primary Habitat: **Nearly endemic to California**, these birds have one of the smallest ranges of any bird in North America. They nest in the vicinity of fresh water, especially marshy areas, wetlands, and grasslands The most favored sites for colonies are where there are heavy growths of cattails and tules that they can use as substrates for their nests. Populations can be seen in the Yolo Bypass Wildlife Area, Conaway Ranch, the Consumnes River Preserve and the Sacramento National Wildlife Refuge.

Males are larger than females and possess dark red shoulder patches trimmed with white on the wings, giving the species its name. (They are often confused with Red-Winged Blackbirds which have a yellow margin rather than white.) Females are brown and look like large sparrows. These birds breed in large colonies that can sometimes reach up to 50,000. For more information about these birds, see the U.C. Davis Tricolored Blackbird Portal online at: http://tricolor.ice.ucdavis.edu/

Primary Threat(s): Loss of habitat, pesticide poisoning, human disturbance, climate change, changes in agriculture, and water usage practices. According to the Audubon Society's website, "*In more recent years, the species has become dependent on agricultural lands, with most of the largest colonies nesting in grain fields. A real dilemma develops because Tricolored young typically have not yet left the nest before the time farmers harvest their crop, and harvesting destroys Tricolored Blackbird nests and young. In some cases as many as 20,000 nests have been lost in a single field.*" Some farmers have employed the use of harvesting machines that can locate the birds' nests and avoid them. Efforts are taking place throughout the state through both environmental and agricultural groups to come to a solution to better protect the birds.

In December of 2014 an emergency petition requesting that the birds be listed as federally "Endangered" because their numbers have declined by over 87% since the 1930's was temporarily granted. However, after the review period ended, the birds were not placed on the federal "Endangered" list.

Tree Swallow *(Tachycineta bicolor)*

Photo by Mary K. Hanson.

Primary Habitat: Fields, marshes, riparian areas, shorelines, wooded swamps and beaver ponds. They prefer to live near bodies of water that produce a lot of flying insects (for food), with adjacent sites where the birds can nest. These Swallows cannot excavate their own nesting cavities and need existing ones in which to raise their young. Natural cavities have been disappearing as people clear the land, manage woodlands, cut down older trees, and remove dead trees, so man-made nesting boxes are of a great help to them.

Species is "Secure" at This Time

Primary Threat(s): Loss of nesting cavities, degradation of habitat, insecticide use, climate change. Tree Swallows are common but their populations declined between 1966 and 2010, resulting in a cumulative drop of 36%, according to the North American Breeding Bird Survey. According to Audubon's climate model, Tree Swallows will soon be wintering farther north and farther inland. The model predicts a 56% loss of current winter range.

Western Bluebird *(Sialia mexicana)*

Male Western Bluebird. Photo by Mary K. Hanson.

Species is "Secure" at This Time

Primary Habitat: Low-elevation pine and mixed forests, rich riparian bottomlands, savanna, open woodlands and at the edges of woods. They often in thrive in areas where the forest has been burned and there is an abundance of dead trees to nest in. They cannot excavate their own nesting cavities and depend on other birds to provide them or on pre-existing holes in dead trees.

Males are brilliant blue with a pink blush on the breast; females are more subtly washed with blue and pink.

According to the Yolo Audubon Society: *"A preferred food for this species is mistletoe berries; the elimination of mistletoe or the larger and older oaks that contain that parasitic plant can eliminate this species from a region."*

Primary Threat(s): Loss of habitat; human interference (when old trees are removed); competition for nesting sites and food by invasive species like the European Starling.

Western Grebe, "Swan Neck Grebe" (Aechmophorus occidentalis)

Western Grebe with courtship weeds, taken near Clearlake, CA. Photo by Sylvia Wright.

Species is "Secure" at This Time

Primary Habitat: Wetland areas, fresh water and brackish marshes, lakes and reservoirs, extensive areas of open water bordered by vegetation (such as rushes and tules). These birds are migratory. They're most known for their dramatic courtship displays during which the birds rush across the water in choreographed routines with their long necks extended.

Although categorized as a federal and global "Species of Least Concern", there have been calls and reports submitted asking that this species be put on the federal Birds of Conservation Concern list and the California Bird Species of Special Concern list. Audubon California in 2010 launched a project to protect breeding Western Grebes at four lakes, including Clear Lake.

Primary Threat(s): Loss of habitat, human disturbance (house-boating around breeding pairs is an issue), water management practices, water pollution, climate change, drought, heavy metal contamination, disease. Audubon's climate model projects a 96% loss of current summer range by 2080.

Western Kingbird (Tyrannus verticalis)

Species is "Secure" at This Time

Primary Habitat: Preferred habitats include grasslands, savannah, pastures, cultivated fields, and urban land; often live near the edges of woodlands. They may be found near Fremont cottonwood, Arizona sycamore, oaks, junipers, cottonwoods, and ponderosa pine. They can be found in farmland throughout the region, especially in Yolo County and at the Bufferlands in Sacramento County.

When threatened, the Kingbird can become very aggressive and scold or chase intruders (including large birds of prey) clapping its bill. It will also flash the crimson feathers it normally hides under its gray crown.

Primary Threat(s): This adaptable bird seems to do well in areas where humans are present as long as they have suitable habitat available to them. The major threat to them is insecticide poisoning. Western Kingbirds are common and have been increasing slightly across most of their breeding range since 1966, according to the North American Breeding Bird Survey.

Western Kingbird. Photo by Ron Dudley.

Western Meadowlark *(Sturnella neglecta)*

Photo by Mary K. Hanson

Species is "Secure" at This Time

Primary Habitat: grasslands, prairies, meadows, pastures, wetland regions, and along marsh edges. Regionally, they can often be found in the Yolo Bypass Wildlife Area, the Sacramento National Wildlife Refuge, and the Cosumnes River Preserve. They can also be found singing on fences along the highways throughout the Central Valley.

The Western Meadowlark is a colorful member of the blackbird family, and are known for their clear, loud, cheery songs. This bird has a brilliant yellow breast with a distinctive black "V"-shape band. They feed by "gaping", using their strong bills to open up hole in the ground and vegetation to get at insects other birds cannot reach. Meadowlarks are sometimes called "Walking Birds" for their penchant to walk along the ground in a stout upright position. Males are "bigamists", having two mates at the same time. Females nest on the ground, and can sometimes be found nesting in depressions in the ground made by cows in grazing areas. In 1914, grain growers did the earliest studies of the Meadowlark and found that although the Meadowlarks do eat grain, they are also experts at insect control and were more beneficial to croplands than they were a nuisance.

Primary Threat(s): conversion of breeding areas for agricultural use, harassment by humans, pesticides, habitat degradation due to invasive plant species.

White Pelican, American White Pelican *(Pelecanus erythrorhynchos)*

Species is "Secure" at This Time

White Pelicans and Double-Crested Cormorants in Clearlake, CA. by Sylvia Wright.

Primary Habitat: Fresh water lakes and ephemeral islands in shallow wetlands. They forage in shallow water on inland marshes, along the edges of lakes or rivers, and in wetlands, commonly 30 miles or more from their nesting islands. During migrations, they stop in similar habitats to forage and rest.

White Pelicans migrate through our region with wintering stop-offs at the Yolo Basin, Clear Lake, the Sacramento National Wildlife Preserve and the Consumnes River Preserve, among other places.

Primary Threat(s): Human disturbance, destruction of foraging and breeding habitat, water management.

White-Breasted Nuthatch *(Sitta carolinensis)*

Primary Habitat: old-growth open deciduous or mixed forest, including orchards, parks, suburban gardens and cemeteries; open montane pine-oak woodlands; Pinyon-juniper and riverside woodlands. The presence of mature or decaying trees with holes suitable for nesting is essential. These birds can be found along Putah Creek and Cache Creek, in the riparian areas near the American and Sacramento Rivers, and other similar areas.

This nuthatch is sometimes called the "Upside Down Bird" for its penchant to hang upside down from branches and tree trunks. *It is protected under the Migratory Bird Treaty Act of 1918.*

Species is "Secure" at This Time

White-Breasted Nuthatch building a nest. Photo by Mary K. Hanson.

Primary Threat(s): Competition for nesting sites with invasive species; loss of habitat. The removal of dead trees from forests may cause problems locally for this species because it requires cavity sites for nesting. Audubon's climate model forecasts a 78 percent loss of current summer range by 2080, with substantial range shift northward.

Wood Ducks *(Aix sponsa)*

Primary Habitat: These ducks live and breed around streams, lakes, freshwater marshes, wetland areas and beaver ponds with tall trees nearby. They nest in trees (in holes left behind by other birds or squirrels, or in manmade nesting boxes) up to 50 feet off the ground. Regionally, these ducks can be found in the Yolo Bypass Wildlife Area, Lake Solano, Lake Berryessa, Clear Lake, the Sacramento National Wildlife Preserve, the Cosumnes River Preserve, and sometimes in city parks throughout Sacramento County, among other places. Nesting pairs are also found at Conway Ranch in Yolo County which provides the birds with nesting boxes.

According to Cornell's "All About Birds" website: *"... They are one of the few duck species equipped with strong claws that can grip bark and perch on branches...."* Then the ducklings are old enough to leave the nest, they often have to make a horrific jump to the ground to meet up with their mother, but because they are so light, the ducklings are seldom injured from the fall and usually just bounce softly on the ground.

Primary Threat(s): These ducks were brought to the edge of extinction in the late 19th century due to habitat loss and over-hunting (The males make handsome trophies.) Current population are now stable, however, and seem to be on the rise thanks to the introduction of man-made nest boxes. Wood ducks still face the threat of human interference with nesting sites, drainage of wetland areas, and poaching. Predators also take their toll on Wood Ducks. At the Conaway Ranch, there were problems one year with Black-Crowned Night Herons who attacked the Wood Duck nesting boxes on the ranch and decimated half of the brooding females, their eggs and their chicks.

Male and female Wood Ducks. Photo by Mary K. Hanson

Yellow-Breasted Chat *(Icteria virens)*

Public Domain Photo from Creative Commons, Phil Myers.

Primary Habitat: The Yellow-Breasted Chat inhabits riparian thickets of willow and other brushy tangles near water. They can also be found in dense deciduous and coniferous forests, along streams, swamps, forest edges, regenerating burned forests, and upland thickets. They can often be found in Rumsey and Woodland in Yolo County, and in Sacramento. They have also been regularly spotted along Putah Creek (near the Monticello Dam), along Cache Creek near the County Road 89 bridge, and on the Sacramento River at the Elk Horn Slough.

Despite its bright coloring, it's often overlooked because of its penchant to "skulk" around brushy habitats. Its eggs are white or off-white with speckling, and there are usually up to 6 in a clutch.

Primary Threat(s): Loss of riparian habitat due to agriculture and expanding development.

California Sepcies of Special Concern

Yellow-Headed Blackbird *(Xanthocephalus xanthocephalus)*

California Sepcies of Special Concern

Primary Habitat: breed almost exclusively in marshes with tall emergent vegetation, such as tules or cattails, generally in open areas and edges over relatively deep water. The birds breed throughout the Berryessa Snow Mountain region from Sacramento County and Yolo County up to Colusa County. There is a large population (about 100 nesting sites) around Clear Lake in Lake County.

Its call has been described as "a rusty farm gate opening". When feeding in large flocks, the birds at the head of the line pick up seeds and then the row behind them leap-frogs over the leaders to feed. The flock keeps moving forward in this way until everyone is sated.

Primary Threat(s): Loss of habitat, water management, climate change, drought. Aerial-applied pesticides may drift into breeding colonies, potentially causing nestling mortality. Some studies indicate that the "...90% loss of historic wetlands in the Central Valley (Frayer et al. 1989) has likely had a large adverse effect on the breeding abundance of this species in this region..."

Audubon's climate model projects a 68 percent loss of current summer range by 2080, with the current winter range suffering a similar 64 percent decline.

Female Yellow-Headed Blackbird being readied for release after banding at Conaway Ranch, Yolo County, CA. Photo by Sylvia Wright.

Arrowhead Blue Butterfly *(Glaucopsyche piasus)*

Arrowhead Blue Butterfly. Photo by Tom Murray.

Listed by NatureServe as Critically Imperiled – a species at very high risk of extinction due to extreme rarity (often 5 or fewer populations), very steep declines, or other factors.

Primary Habitat: Found in the Western US and Canada, this rarely seen butterfly's habitat preferences are not well understood. It occurs in rocky canyons and mixed mesic forest at mid-elevation, and also at or near the tree-line. It is always found near perennial lupines. Females lay eggs on the lupine's flower buds and caterpillars feed on its flowers and fruits. Males patrol during the day near the host plants. There are several similar-looking species, but this one can be identified by the heavy underside pattern on its wings.

This butterfly may be seen throughout much of the region in small numbers wherever native lupine is growing.

Primary Threat(s): Unknown.

Bison Snake-Tail Dragonfly *(Ophiogomphus bison)*

Primary Habitat: In the foothills and lower mountain zones along the margins of creeks, rivers, and lakes. Most visible between May and August. In California there are about 113 different species of *Odonates*, and what's extra special for those of us who live in the counties encompassing the Berryessa Snow Mountain region is the fact that almost <u>half</u> of those species live right here!

Species is "Secure" at This Time

All Bison Snake-Tails are migratory, but you may find these dragonflies along the creeks and rivers in the region, sitting on rocks waiting for females, as they migrate through in the late summer.

There are only four species of snake-tail in California, and the Bison is the darkest in color. The name "snake-tail" is derived from the shape of the end of this dragonfly's tail which is broad at the base and looks like the hooded head of a cobra.

One of the most prominent features of the dragonfly is its set of huge multi-faceted eyes. The eyes have as many as 30,000 separate lenses. Most dragonflies have broad-spectrum color vision and can even see into the ultraviolet range.

Primary Threat(s): loss of habitat, water pollution, human disturbance, water management, climate change.

Bison Snake-Tail Dragonfly. Photo by Mary K. Hanson.

Black Saddlebags Dragonfly *(Tramea lacerata)*

Photo by Mary K. Hanson

Species is "Secure" at This Time

Primary Habitat: Marshy ponds, wetland areas, lakes, ditches, and slow streams and creeks, preferably with a year-round water supply. They like their breeding ponds a little brackish, calm and warm.

This dragonfly is relatively large and has conspicuous iridescent-black patches on the inside margins of its otherwise clear wings. The males are equipped with a brush-like appendage on the end of their tail that they can use to "brush out" the sperm of other males if they come across a female that has already been mated. There can be two generations of the dragonflies breeding in the same year.

Males often collect for feeding frenzies when there are large enough quantities of insects for them to eat. (Females do not form or join in these groups, however.) In 2013 large swarms of feeding males were found all along I-5 from Redding in Shasta County to Woodland in Yolo County, according to a Migratory Dragonfly Partnership report.

Primary Threat(s): loss of habitat, water pollution, human disturbance, water management, climate change.

Columbian Skipper *(Hesperia columbia)*

Listed by NatureServe as Vulnerable – a species at moderate risk of extinction or elimination due to a restricted range, relatively few populations, recent and widespread declines, or other factors.

Primary Habitat: This butterfly prefers rocky, hilly areas and is found mainly in the California Coast Range. It is also found in chaparral and serpentine areas. Caterpillars feed on native bunchgrasses.

You may be able to see these skimmers throughout the Cedar Roughs Wilderness and along Walker Ridge where there are large outcroppings of serpentine, and in the Lagoon Valley Regional Park in Vacaville.

Like all skippers this one combines the characteristics of both butterflies and moths. Most skippers hold their wings at different angles over their fuzzy moth-like bodies, sometimes upright like butterflies, sometimes horizontally like moths, and their antenna terminate in "knobs". Its very unusual underside pattern makes this uncommon skipper easy to identify.

Primary Threat(s): Unknown, but most likely expanding development and invasive plant species.

© 2010 Kim Davis & Mike Stangeland * http://kimandmikeontheroad.com/

Common Buckeye Butterfly *(Junonia coenia)*

Species is "Secure" at This Time

Primary Habitat: Forest margins, wet meadows, old fields, gardens, riparian areas, open fields, pastures, roadsides, pineland, disturbed sites. It is fond of open, sunny locations with low-growing vegetation. Host plants include toadflax, snapdragons, False Foxglove, plantain and twinflower. Adults feed on nectar and also take fluids from mud and damp sand. They can usually be found close to their food sources, and sometimes drink out of mud puddles.

This is a relatively small butterfly, and the large iridescent eyespots on the wings are used to startle predators, especially birds.

Their eggs are dark green and are usually laid in small groupings. Caterpillars range from light colors with orange-brown splotches to black and have black branched spines poking out of them. The head is orange with short black and white protuberances on it.

Primary Threat(s): Loss of habitat, herbicide and insecticide use.

Butterfly Photo by Mary K. Hanson. Caterpillar photo is a Public Domain Image from http://freepages.misc.rootsweb.ancestry.com/

Common Whitetail Skimmer Dragonfly *(Libellula lydia)*

Primary Habitat: Found at ponds, marshes and meadows throughout the region. Older males develop a white powdery coloring on their bodies ("pruinosity"), which is most evident in this species. (Females are brown with white spots.) They can often be found along the margins of Lake Berryessa, Lake Solano, and Clear Lake, and in the wetlands region of the Yolo Bypass Wildlife Area.

Species is "Secure" at This Time

Fairly large dragonflies, they're sometimes referred to as "King Skimmers". These dragonflies "perch" on objects near the water and "hawk" for mosquitoes and other small insects to eat. They can become very aggressive during mating season. Like all dragonflies, they spend their early life under water as voracious nyads. This species only lives for about 36 days after emerging as full-grown dragonflies. Dragonflies are among the most ancient creatures on the planet, and can trace their ancestry back over 300-million years to Carboniferous times.

Primary Threat(s): Loss of habitat, water pollution, expanding development, water management.

Public Domain Photo from http://www.public-domain-image.com/

Edith's Checkerspot Butterfly *(Euphydryas editha)*

Edith's Checkerspot. Photo by Tom Murray and www.bugguide.net.
Caterpillar photo by Owen Holt and www.bugguide.net

Listed by NatureServe as Vulnerable – a species at moderate risk of extinction or elimination due to a restricted range, relatively few populations, recent and widespread declines, or other factors.

Primary Habitat: It can be found from sea level to the tree-line through diverse habitats including chaparral, meadows, fields, foothills, open woods, and alpine fell-fields.

Locally, it can be seen in serpentine areas visiting puddles and flowers and it always occurs as very localized colonies. Caterpillars feed on members of the Snapdragon and Plantain families.

Primary Threat(s): Unknown, but most likely expanding development; loss of habitat.

Two subspecies (*Bay Checkerspot* and *Quino Checkerspot*) are listed as Federally Endangered. The National Academy of Sciences says the *Quino* "is the first endangered species for which climate change is officially listed as both a current threat and a factor to be considered in the plan for its recovery..."

Gray Hairstreak Butterfly *(Strymon melinus)*

Species is "Secure" at This Time

Primary Habitat: One of the most common hairstreaks in the country it can be found almost everywhere in the United States. The Gray Hairstreak prefers open areas, fields, meadows, parks and lush garden areas, and does well is "disturbed" areas. It has a very broad variety of host plants, including milkweed, Queen Anne's Lace, Cow Vetch, Goldenrod, and a variety of other flowering plants.

A small butterfly, it's most visible in our region between May and September, and has two breeding cycles. Caterpillars are pale pink and grey with a light layer of fuzz.

The most interesting feature of this small butterfly are the large bight eye-spots near its extra-thin hair-like tails that extend from the end of the back wings. When sitting on a flower, it's not uncommon for these butterflies to make their tail extensions waggle slightly by rubbing their wings backwards and forwards.

Primary Threat(s): Insecticide use.

Photo by Mary K. Hanson

Gray Marble Butterfly *(Anthocharis lanceolata)*

Listed by NatureServe as Vulnerable – a species at moderate risk of extinction or elimination due to a restricted range, relatively few populations, recent and widespread declines, or other factors.

Primary Habitat: This butterfly is scattered through the mountains of California, and can also be found in Oregon and Nevada.

It is generally scarce and local.

Typical habitats include south slopes of wooded, walled canyons, and mountain ravines that possess suitable caterpillar host plants.

Host plants include native mustards (*Brassicaceae*) and Jewel Flowers (*Streptanthus*). The caterpillars eat the leaves as well as the buds/flowers/fruit of their host plants.

Primary Threat(s): There is insufficient information to evaluate threats this species is facing, but it is most likely threatened by expanding development, invasive species, grazing, insecticide use, and fire.

Photo by Ray Bruun and www.bugguide.net

Indra Swallowtail Butterfly, "Cliff Swallowtail" *(Papilio indra)*

Listed by NatureServe as Apparently Secure – a species that is uncommon but not rare; there is some cause for long-term concern due to declines or other factors.

Primary Habitat: This butterfly is found in bare, rocky areas in mountains, including mountains and canyons, where it can be seen visiting puddles. **In the Berryessa Snow Mountain region, it is found on serpentine at low elevations. Caterpillars were spotted on the Pope-to-Putah Trail in 2015.**

The butterflies are black with yellow markings. Caterpillars go through several instars, and at the final stage are striped black and pink. They feed on herbs of the parsley family.

Primary Threat(s): The greatest threat to these butterflies is the removal of the brightly colored caterpillars from public lands. *Permits are now required to remove specimens from federal public lands.*

A Pair of Indra Swallowtails. Public Domain Photo from http://www.public-domain-image.com/. Caterpillar photo is a Public Domain Photo from Creative Commons.

Leather Oak Duskywing *(Erynnis brizo lacustra)*

Primary Habitat: This narrowly distributed **endemic** butterfly is **restricted to serpentine soils in** the Coast Range and Sierra Nevada foothills, where its only known host plant is Leather Oak or Serpentine Scrub Oak (*Quercus durata*). It can be seen visiting puddles and twisting into and among leather oak thickets… magically going into one, but coming out of another! Their eggs are "squatty" and white with ribbed sides.

There are a number of species in the genus *Erynnis* in the Berryessa Snow Mountain region. They are notoriously difficult to identify, but this is the only one strongly restricted to serpentine areas.

Species is "Secure" at This Time

© 2010 Kim Davis & Mike Stangeland * http://kimandmikeontheroad.com/

Primary Threat(s): Unknown, but most likely expanding development.

Lindsey's Skipper *(Hesperia lindseyi)*

Listed by NatureServe as Vulnerable – a species at moderate risk of extinction or elimination due to a restricted range, relatively few populations, recent and widespread declines, or other factors.

Primary Habitat: This uncommon butterfly is largely restricted to **serpentine grassland** in our area, usually in places where there is a large display of *Clarkia* (native annual herbs with pink or purple flowers). It ranges from Oregon south to Riverside County in California. There are four subspecies of this skipper in California.

Adults fly low, near the ground, and often sit on bare ground. Caterpillars feed on native perennial grasses. Females lay eggs haphazardly on a variety of different plants including lupine, but will also lay eggs on the pale green lichen *(Usnea)* that growns on trees. The eggs overwinter and the caterpillars feed on leaves (sheltering themselves with leaves tied together with silk).

This skipper has a very short fly period, usually between June 15th to July 15th.

Note: The common Sandhill Skipper, *Polites sabuleti,* is marked very similarly but is decidedly smaller.

Primary Threat(s): Unknown, but likely expanding development.

Lindsey's Skipper. Photo from http://www.adamwiner.com/

Monarch Butterfly *(Danaus plexippus)*

In late 2014, three conservation organizations and a noted scientist asked the U.S. Fish & Wildlife Service to protect the monarch butterfly and list it as a "Federally Threatened Species". As of the writing of this guide that status is pending.

According to Monarch Watch.com: *"(We are) engaged...in discussions about how to provide more habitat for monarchs. The White House supports these initiatives..."*

Primary Habitat: In the spring and summer, the monarch butterfly's habitat is open fields, gardens and meadows with **milkweed**. The Central Valley sees Monarchs in the late summer and early fall as they migrate south to Mexico. Although more commonly seen along the coast, some migrating Monarchs do come further inland throughout the Berryessa Snow Mountain region. According to the World Wildlife Fund, *"The Monarch butterfly exhibits the most highly evolved migration pattern of any known species of butterfly or moth and perhaps any known insect."* The WWF 2013 report from Mexico showed that the number of monarch butterflies wintering there was at its lowest in 20 years. In 2015 The Sacramento National Wildlife Refuge started a milkweed garden, and was successful in bringing Monarchs into to the preserve.

Primary Threat(s): The primary threats to the monarch butterfly include the loss of milkweed (the Monarchs' only host plant); degradation of overwintering sites; drought, and climate change. Loss of milkweed is primarily due to the dramatic increase in the use of the herbicide Roundup™ according to the Xerces Society. *"The large-scale use of systemic insecticides such as neonicotinoids within the breeding range of the monarch poses a considerable threat."*

To assist with the reestablishment of Monarch populations, the Xerces Society encourages everyone to plant native milkweed plants in your yard or along the margins of your agricultural property. To help with that endeavor, **Hedgerow Farms in Winters, CA** has partnered with the Xerces Society to create and sell a forb pollinator seed mix for use in Northern California. This mix, along with three different varieties of milkweed seeds, is available in large quantities ($100 minimum) by calling Hedgerow Farms directly at 530-662-6847 or info@hedgerow farms.com. Smaller packets of the Hedgerow seeds mixes are also available for order online through **Larner Seed** at www.larnerseeds.com at a nominal cost. The **California Native Plant Society** may also have seeds and plants available at their nursery. For more information see their website at: www.sacvalleycnps.org.

Photos by Mary K. Hanson.

Mormon Metalmark Butterfly *(Apodemia mormo)*

Mormon Metalmark Butterfly. Public Domain Photo from http://www.public-domain-image.com/ Caterpillar photo is a Public Domain Image from Creative Commons courtesy of Nicky Davis.

Listed by NatureServe as Secure – a species that is common, widespread, and abundant.

Primary Habitat: This butterfly is found from sea level to 7,000 feet in a variety of mostly open, rocky habitats in the Western US. Its flight is very distinctive – it wheels in circles and often does figure-eights, and it is very "nervous" on flowers, keeping its wings in constant motion. It flies in autumn and always occurs in association with perennial Wild Buckwheat species *(Eriogonum)*, its host plant.

Several colonies have been found in the Mendocino National Forest.

Primary Threat(s): habitat loss, invasive plant species, expanding development.

Muir's Hairstreak Butterfly *(Callophrys muiri)*

Listed by NatureServe as Imperiled – a species at high risk of extinction or elimination due to very restricted range, very few populations, steep declines, or other factors.

Primary Habitat: It prefers hilly, rocky, serpentine areas, where it feeds on nectar from wild lilac and other flowers. The butterfly will **lay its eggs only on Sargent Cypress** (*Cupressus sargentii*) trees. And the caterpillars feed on Sargent Cypress and MacNab's Cypress (*Cupressus macnabiana*). Adults can be found perched on cypress trees and at mud puddles in early spring.

This butterfly is found in California's Coastal Mountains from San Luis Obispo County north to Mendocino County. **It is particularly found in the Cedar Roughs Wilderness area within the Berryessa Snow Mountain region where there is the largest stand of Sargent Cypress in the world, and along Walker Ridge.**

Primary Threat(s): habitat loss.

© 2008 Kim Davis & Mike Stangeland * http://www.kimandmikeontheroad.com/

Neon Skimmer Dragonfly *(Libellula croceipennis)*

Neon Skimmer (female). Photo by Mary K. Hanson.

Species is "Secure" at This Time

Primary Habitat: This species prefers clean slow-moving streams and flowing ditches, usually wooded but sometimes in the open. Also found in garden ponds and wetland areas where there are permanent ponds in which to lay their eggs. Regionally it can be found around the Yolo Bypass Wildlife Area, the Cache Creek Nature Preserve, Lake Solano, Clear Lake, and the Cosumnes River Preserve, among other places.

According to Bugguide.net: *"Compared to other red dragonflies in the area, male Neon Skimmers are larger and 'glow' in the sun; females are golden-colored in sunlight but may look duller tan on cloudy days or in shade. Very strong flyers, relatively bold and easy to photograph."* Female Neon Skimmers are identifiable from the males by the white stripe down the back.

Primary Threat(s): Loss of habitat, water pollution, expanding development, water management.

Northern Bluet Damselfly *(Enallagma annexum)*

Species is "Secure" at This Time

Primary Habitat: From June to August, these damselflies occupy lakes, ponds, and marshes, and streams with slow to moderate flow. The species occurs in a wide variety of habitats, from sagebrush to mountain lakes. Males are blue; females are greenish to yellow-brown. Regionally, these common damselflies can be found along the shores of Putah and Cache Creek, Lake Solano, Lake Berryessa, the Cache Creek Nature Preserve, the Yolo Bypass Wildlife Area, and other places.

Northern Bluet Damselfly. Image from bugguide.net

Damselflies differ from dragonflies in size (they are generally much smaller), and whereas dragonflies hold their wings out while resting, most damselflies hold their wings against their sides or on their backs. Unlike some damselflies, the female Bluet cuts a hole in submerged vegetation and carefully lays her eggs in it.

Primary Threat(s): Populations are widespread, abundant, and secure. Like all water-dependent insects, however, damselflies can be affected by water management practices, drought, water pollution and climate change.

Oreas Comma Butterfly, "Oreas Angelwing" *(Polygonia oreas)*

Public Domain Photo from iNaturalist.org by Bill Bouton.

Listed by NatureServe as Vulnerable – a species at moderate risk of extinction or elimination due to a restricted range, relatively few populations, recent and widespread declines, or other factors.

Primary Habitat: Coastal canyons, streamsides, redwood and other conifer forests mostly where gooseberries (*Ribes* species) -- the caterpillars' host plants -- are common. In the Berryessa Snow Mountain region, this butterfly is rare but has been spotted on Goat Mountain and at Letts Lake in the Mendocino National Forest.

The butterflies' wings have sharp distinct borders and yellow chevron markings along the submargins. Their eggs are green with pale stripes running top to bottom. The dark gray caterpillars feed on gooseberry plants, and the adult butterflies take in the juices from the rotting fruit and tree sap (seldom flower nectar.) Their flights are usually between June and October.

Primary Threat(s): Unknown, but loss of habitat is highly suspected.

Painted Lady Butterfly *(Vanessa cardui)*

Species is "Secure" at This Time

Primary Habitat: The Painted Lady inhabits backyards and meadows throughout most of the world. An irruptive migrant, this is a species that occasionally migrates without regard to geography or season. Generally, they inhabit open meadows and fields, disturbed areas and roadsides, and any sunny place that provides appropriate nectar and host plants (such as thistles, American Elm, Black Cherry, English Plantain, and daisies). Regionally, a common butterfly, it is found almost everywhere including the Davis Arboretum, along Cache and Putah Creek, and in household gardens.

The eggs are pale green and barrel-shaped. Caterpillars are black with yellow markings, and they grow over an inch long before they turn to pupae. Adult butterflies live for about 20 days, but can travel great distances and fly at a speed of up to 30 miles per hour.

This is a butterfly is one that is commonly used in "butterfly kits" that can be purchased on the internet.

Primary Threat(s): Unknown

Painted Lady Butterfly. Photo by Mary K. Hanson. Caterpillar photo is a Public Domain Image from Creative Commons

Pipevine Swallowtail Butterfly *(Battus philenor hirsuta)*

Pipevine Swallowtail Butterfly, caterpillar and chrysalis. Photos by Mary K. Hanson.

Primary Habitat: A subspecies of the common Pipevine Swallowtails, *Battus philenor hirsute* is **endemic to Northern California**. Populations are found throughout the Sacramento Valley and outside of the valley in Contra Costa and Alameda Counties. They can be found in riparian or forested areas, parks and gardens where there is an abundance of their host plant: pipevine (*Aristolochia*). An extremely large population can be found at the American River Bend Park in Sacramento County in the spring. Hundreds of butterflies and caterpillars can be found congregating in and around the area between March and May. In the Berryessa Snow Mountain region, they can be found along Putah and Cache Creek, Lake Solano, Lake Berryessa, and Clear Lake and other creeks where the pipevines are present. The pipevine plants are full of a toxin called *aristolochic acid*, and the caterpillars and butterflies retain high concentrations of this toxin in their bodies.

Species is "Secure" at This Time

The butterflies are black with an iridescent blue oversheen (which is more prominent on the males than the females). The caterpillars are reddish-brown when young but turn black with bright orange spikes as they mature.

Primary Threat(s): loss of habitat and host plants. Although they will take nectar from a variety of flower, Pipevine Swallowtail Butterflies are exceedingly "host-specific" when it comes to reproduction. Females will <u>only</u> lay eggs on native pipevine plants and caterpillars will <u>only</u> eat the pipevine. Where the pipvines are removed or destroyed, the butterflies die out. You can coax populations to visit your garden by planting native pipevines.

Scarab-Hunter Wasp *(Campsomeris tolteca)*

Species is "Secure" at This Time

Primary Habitat: An adaptive insect the Scarab-Hunter can live in a variety of environments including riparian habitats and grasslands. Temperature is the greatest determining factor. These wasps like it warm. They can be found from Texas to California and as far south as Mexico. Males are more slender and elongated than females, with longer antennae.

Locally they can often be found along the American and Sacramento Rivers and their tributaries.

Scarab-Hunters are parasitic wasps and are major source of natural control for the pest Japanese beetle. Females can often be seen hovering over the ground and digging in the dirt for beetle grubs. The female lays her eggs on the grubs, and when the eggs hatch the immature wasps eat the grubs alive. Despite the "murderous" nature of their offspring, mature Scarab Hunters are not carnivorous and get their nourishment from nectar.

Scarab-Hunter Wasp. Photo by Mary K. Hanson.

Primary Threat(s): The major threat to these wasps is pesticide use which kills the wasps and their host-beetles.

Valley Carpenter Bee *(Xylocopa varipuncta)*

Primary Habitat: Valleys and foothills with deciduous trees such as oaks. It is one of three kinds of **native** carpenter bees in California, and is named for the Central Valley where it is most-often found. There is a large population that regularly visits the Häagen-Dazs Honey Bee Haven adjacent to the Harry H. Laidlaw Jr. Honey Bee Research Facility at U. C. Davis. Native pollinator specialist Robbin Thorp, emeritus professor of entomology at UCD, calls the stingless male Valley Carpenter Bee "the teddy bear bee."

Species is "Secure" at This Time

They are called "carpenter" bees because the females excavate tunnels in weathered unpainted wood (trees, telephone poles, fences, etc.) using their mandibles (but they don't ingest the wood). The bees overwinter as adults in the tunnels and emerge in the spring.

This is the largest **native** bee in California, and there is no other *Xylocopa* that is so sexually dimorphic. The females are pure black and shiny, and the males are fuzzy, golden and have green eyes (like the one in the photo). Males are most often seen in the late afternoon showing off in the sunlight. Like most native bees, Carpenter Bees are solitary and do not form hives or have "queens". They spend most of their life in their tunnels, so they're usually only seen in flight during the spring.

Primary Threat(s): Insecticide use.

Valley Carpenter Bee (male). Photo by Mary K. Hanson.

Snakefly *(Raphidiidae (Genus Agulla))*

Female Snakefly. Photo by Mary K. Hanson.

Primary Habitat: There are over 200 different species of snakeflies, and although they are common in Europe, in the United States they can only be found in the western states. In California they can be found throughout the Berryessa Snow Mountain region in all types of forests (up to the timberline).

Species is "Secure" at This Time

Beneficial predators, snakeflies eat pest insect eggs and larva, small insects, and pollen. They are distinguished by the elongated "neck" (prothorax) and large compound eyes. Females (like the one in our photo) have a long, thin ovipositor, but they do not sting. Eggs are laid in the bark of trees and it can take two years or more for the larvae to mature.

Primary Threat(s): insecticide and herbicide use that kills the flies, their food sources and the trees in which they lay their eggs.

Tiger Swallowtail Butterfly, Western Tiger Swallowtail *(Papilio rutulus)*

Species is "Secure" at This Time

Primary Habitat: This is a common butterfly found throughout northern California, especially near woodland streams and rivers, canyons, and riparian areas. They can also be found in suburban gardens where their favorite plants and trees are in abundance (such as cottonwood, willow, aspen, California Buckeye, thistles, zinnias and yerba santa.) It's not uncommon to see these butterflies along Cache Creek, Putah Creek, the American and Sacramento Rivers and their tributaries, and other riparian areas.

Adult butterflies are distinguished by their large black-and-yellow striped wings and bodies, with iridescent blue eye-spots at the lower margin of the swallow-tail. Males can often be found congregating alongside creeks and streams, drinking from the water and extracting minerals from the mud. Females can lay up to 100 deep-green eggs (which they lay singly on the underside of leaves). The caterpillars go through several molts (instars) and change drastically in appearance from one instar to the next. In early instars they look like blobs of bird droppings, but later develop into green caterpillars with large bright eye spots on the rear,

Primary Threat(s): broad spectrum insecticides.

Photo by Mary K. Hanson

Tussock Moth Caterpillar, Western Tussock Moth Caterpillar *(Orgyia vetusta)*

Caterpillar photo by Mary K. Hanson. Female moth and cocoon photo by Hartmut Wisch

Primary Habitat: There are over 300 different kinds of Tussock Moths, but this one is found only in the western states, and mostly in California throughout oak woodland areas. In our area, they are often found wherever hardwood trees are growing, especially oak trees in the late spring and early summer. Caterpillars build cocoons in part out of their own hair, and overwinter in them until spring.

Species is "Secure" at This Time

The male moths are rather drab (with brown patterned wings and bodies), but the females are pale gray and are <u>wingless</u>. Females emerge from their cocoons and emit a pheromone which attracts the males to them. The caterpillars are very distinctive with a black stripe flanked by broad yellow stripes, four tufts of hair (yellowish, grey or white), and red "glands" from which other hairs protrude.

CAUTION: The hairs on the caterpillar may cause an allergic reaction in some people.

Primary Threat(s): insecticide and herbicide use. Considered something of a "pest", the moths feed on foliage and young fruit, but they are usually kept in check by natural larval parasites (such as *Hyposoter exiguae* and *Dibrachys sp.*) and the predatory carpet beetle (*Trogoderma sternale*).

Valley Elderberry Longhorn Beetle *(Desmocerus californicus dimorphus)*

Federally Threatened

Primary Habitat: This subspecies of longhorn beetle is **native** to California and is found in riparian areas where there is an abundance of the beetles' only host plant: blue elderberry (*Sambucus spp.*). Regionally, they can be found along the American River and Putah Creek in areas where elderberry plants are abundant.

The beetles are exceedingly "host-specific". Females lay eggs in the bark of the elderberry, and when the larva hatch they burrow into the stems. The larva can remain inside the bark for up to 2 years before emerging. Adults can be seen between March and June. The rummaging action of the adult beetles pollinates the flowers of the elderberries and plays a key role in sustaining the elderberry populations.

Primary Threat(s): Loss of host plants and habitat due to development; pesticides; and herbicide use

NOTE: In 2014 there were proposals to have this insect "delisted" from its "threatened" status, but that petition was withdrawn in September 2014. The Department of Fish and Wildlife determined, *"that the threats to the species and its habitat have not been reduced to the point where the species no longer meets the statutory definition of an endangered or threatened species."*

Photo by Mary K. Hanson.

Vivid Dancer Damselfly (*Argia vivida*)

Public Domain Photo from http://commons.wikimedia.org/

Species is "Secure" at This Time

Primary Habitat: Marshes and wetlands; spring-fed streams, seeps, hot and cold springs. They need shade, though, so springs or creeks where there's plentiful shade nearby really attracts these damselflies. Adults usually remain close to the water areas where they emerged. A great spot to find these damselflies in the local area is at or around Lake Solano Park in Winters, CA. They can usually be seen in abundance there throughout April and May.

The Vivid is said to have the "longest flight season" of any dragonfly or damselfly in our region: from April to October. Males are vivid blue, and females are usually tan, although some can take on "andromorphic" male coloring. The easiest way to tell these damselflies from the Northern Bluet is by the backwards pointing black arrowheads between the bands on the abdomen.

Primary Threat(s): Loss of habitat (when wetland areas are drained), water pollution, drought, climate change.

Western Sulphur Butterfly, "Golden Sulphur" (*Colias occidentalis chrysomelas*)

Listed by NatureServe as Imperiled – a species at high risk of extinction or elimination due to very restricted range, very few populations, steep declines, or other factors.

Primary Habitat: This butterfly, a rare subspecies of the more common *Colias occidentalis*, is found along roads, trails, streams, and other openings in conifer forests, woodlands, meadows and fields, and shrub and brush lands through the Pacific Northwest and into British Columbia. It can usually be seen between May and July. The males are bright sulfur yellow with a black trim on the wings, but the females may be pale yellow or greenish-white. Males can usually be seen patrolling areas while females lay eggs singly on host plants. They're strong fliers and not easy to approach. Caterpillars eat perennial lupines, vetch, white sweet clover and sweet peas.

© 2009 Kim Davis, Mike Stangeland & Andrew Warren * http://butterfliesofamerica.com/

They can sometimes be found along Highways 16 and 20, and along Walker Ridge when the wildflowers are in bloom.

Primary Threat(s): Fire suppression, invasive species, improper logging, and over-grazing.

Common Galls in the Region

Most of the galls you see on the oak trees are made by tiny wasps. Each different species of wasp has its own special gall. Galls are formed when the wasp lays its egg in the bark, stem or leaf of the tree and the tree exudes a gall form over and around it. All of the photos taken in Sacramento and Yolo County by Mary K. Hanson.

TOP ROW: "Wooly Leaf Gall" and "Popcorn Gall" (on a blue oak tree). **MIDDLE ROW:** "Spangle Galls" and "Spiny Turban Galls". **BOTTOM ROW:** "Red Cone Galls" and the very common "Oak Apple Galls".

Badger, North American Badger (*Taxidea taxus*)

California Species of Special Concern

Photo by Ron Dudley

Primary Habitat: Badgers can be seen throughout the Berryessa Snow Mountain region in open areas like plains, farmland and at the edge of woods.
Badger populations have decreased significantly in the Central Valley area, with the most sightings being in Napa County.

Dens and burrows, called "setts", are a very important part of the badger's life. A badger usually has lots of different setts which are made up of a labyrinth of tunnels and chambers. Badgers are carnivorous animals and eat mice, voles, gophers and squirrels along with some birds and insects.

Primary Threat(s): Intentional killing of badgers by human beings is a major reason for the decline of badger populations in California. Other factors include: changing land uses resulting from agriculture, urban development, and forest ingrowth and loss of prey species.

Beaver, North American Beaver (*Castor canadensis*)

Species is "Secure" at This Time

Primary Habitat: Streams, rivers, marshes, ponds, and along shorelines of large lakes where there is an ample supply of food (bark from trees like beech, maple, cottonwood, willow birch, alder, and aspen, as well as aquatic vegetation, buds, and roots). Beaver can be found at the Cache Creek Nature Preserve, the Yolo Bypass Wildlife Area, the Bufferlands in Sacramento County, and along Putah Creek among other places.

Beavers and humans often have different ideas about what should be dammed and where. But beavers in streams and rivers increase wetland areas and can improve groundwater recharge, according to an article in Science News. Andrew Fulks, UC Davis Putah Creek Riparian Reserve Manager agrees: *"Beaver are a natural part of the ecosystem, and I'm happy they are out on our creek!"*

Primary Threat(s): Once extremely abundant, this beaver was almost hunted to extinction by European colonialists in the American West. However, over the past century, North American beavers have made a remarkable comeback but still face habitat loss. Beavers are also actively removed from streams, canals, and drainage ditches by humans.

In California a permit is required to kill beaver, and permits are only given if there is "satisfactory evidence of damage or destruction" done by the beaver.

North American Beaver. Photo by Roger Jones.

Black Bear, American Black Bear *(Ursus americanus)*

Public Domain Photo from http://commons.wikimedia.org/

Primary Habitat: Black Bears are mainly found in forested areas with thick ground cover and an abundance of fruits, nuts and vegetation, usually at elevations above 3000 feet. They sometimes forage in fields or meadows. During the winter they hibernate in tree cavities, under rocks or logs, or in banks, caves and culverts. Some of the best places to see black bears in the Berryessa Snow Mountain region are in the Cedar Roughs Wilderness and the Snow Mountain Wilderness Area.

Species is "Secure" at This Time

Black Bears aren't always black; they can also be tan or brown. They are excellent climbers and are very powerful. Female Black Bears ("sows") actually have the ability to "time" the birth of their cubs through a process called "delayed implantation." The female can carry a fertilized egg in her body for several months before allowing it to attach to the womb and grow. **WARNING: Do not feed the bears, do not get between a sow and her cubs..** For more information on how to avoid confrontations with Black Bears see this pamphlet: http://sagehen.ucnrs.org/documents/visitors/wildlife/bear.pdf.

Primary Threat(s): habitat loss, confrontations with humans that lead to the bear's fatality.

Coyote *(Canis latrans)*

Species is "Secure" at This Time

Primary Habitat: Highly adaptable, coyotes once lived primarily in open prairies, but now roam the continent's forests and mountains. As humans take over more and more countryside, coyotes are adapting to living in cities as well. Coyotes can be found throughout the Berryessa Snow Mountain region in oak woodlands and riparian forests, and can be seen foraging on grasslands, pastures and farmland, and meadows.

Coyotes can be aggressively territorial, especially in the late spring and early summer when their pups are born, and will protect their dens, packs and hunting grounds from trespassers when they have to. Normally, coyotes are instinctively wary of humans and will avoid contact with them, but when humans supply the coyotes with food and shelter (garbage and outbuildings) coyotes will quickly lose their fear. A pamphlet on how to deal with wild coyotes in urban areas is offered by the Dept. of Fish and Wildlife as part of their "Keep Me Wild" campaign: http://dfg.ca.gov/keepmewild/coyote.html.

Primary Threat(s): Intentional killing by humans.

In California is it illegal to use leg traps, poisons and other methods of eradication. Furthermore, as of December 3, 2014 the is also illegal for anyone to offer cash prizes as incentives for killing coyotes, bobcats or foxes.

Photo by Roger Jones

Hoary Bat (Lasiurus cinereus)

Species is "Secure" at This Time

Primary Habitat: This bat prefers open habitats with some tree cover. It often uses habitat edges and riparian areas for feeding. In California it's also found in evergreen trees in the mountain regions. During the fall and winter, males and females appear to have "elevational separation": males winter in the foothills and mountains, and the females winter in lowlands and coastal valleys. This is a nocturnal generally solitary bat. Look for it roosting in trees. Males will roost closer to the bottom than females.

"Hoary" refers to the "white frost" coloring on the tips of its brown fur. Hoary Bats generally hunt alone and like to feast on moths. Although it's the largest bat species found in this part of North America, it's actually much smaller than you might imagine. It's body is about the length of your thumb.

Primary Threat(s): Hoary Bats are widespread and secure over much of their range, but deforestation and human disturbance are on-going threats.

Hoary Bat. Photo by Roger Jones.

Humboldt Marten (Martes americana humboldtensis)

Primary Habitat: Extirpated from over 95% of its natural habitat, there are only a few populations left in California (specifically in Humboldt County and parts of Del Norte County), so it's not a frequent visitor to the Berryessa Snow Mountain region, but is sometimes seen as a rarity. Its normal habitat is the coastal redwood zone from the Oregon border south to Sonoma county, and is also associated with late-successional coniferous forests with some canopy openings.

Endangered in California

Martens are members of the weasel family, about the size of a cat. They eat small mammals, birds and berries and have the ability to creep up on porcupines and grab them by the face (to avoid the quills).

Primary Threat(s): Habitat fragmentation and loss due to logging and other forest management activities took away 95% of their range; wildfires are also an issue. Disease, and a shallow gene pool are also threats to these martens. Fewer than 100 are known to exist.

In June of 2014 a petition was filed to get the martens designated as an "Endangered Species". Public hearings on the status were held, and a ruling putting them on the "Endangered" list was approved on June 1, 2015. Previous petitions in 2010 and 2012 failed.

Humboldt Marten. Public Domain Photo from http://upload.wikimedia.org/wikipedia/commons

Jackrabbit, Black-Tailed Jackrabbit *(Lepus californicus)*

Black-Tailed Jackrabbit. Photo by Mary K. Hanson.

Species is "Secure" at This Time

Primary Habitat: Black-Tailed Jackrabbits occupy mixed shrub-grassland terrains, meadows, farmland and sometimes wetland and riparian areas that offer them vegetation for food and cover.

Diet consist of a variety of grasses, coarse leaves, twigs, berries and other plant material. Jackrabbits are "hares", not "rabbits". Whereas baby rabbits (commonly called *bunnies*) are born underground, furless and blind, baby hares (called *leverets*) are born above ground and are fully furred with their eyes open so they can leave the nest and forage on their own very quickly after birth.

Primary Threat(s): intentional killing by humans; insecticide poisoning; herbicide use that destroys the plants on which the jackrabbits forage.

Long-Eared Myotis Bat *(Myotis evotis)*

Federal Species of Special Concern

Primary Habitat: This bat is found in a wide range of habitats, including brush, woodland and forest areas, but is most commonly found in mixed coniferous forests.

Long-Ears are often solitary but can roost in colonies up to 30 individuals. Both sexes use a variety of roost sites, but they usually only use caves as night roosts. In the Pacific Northwest, the variety of female roost sites exceeds that of any other bats in that area. In forest populations, these bats usually roost in large snags in canopy gaps or else in stumps in clear-cut areas.

These bats are thought to migrate short distances between summer and winter ranges. They eat a large number of insects such as beetles, moths, flies, and spiders, and collect them mind-flight or on the ground. They also require a great deal of water, and usually live close to a water source.

Its most dominant feature, of course, are its ears. When laid forward the ears are long enough to extend past the tip of the nose. This bat's flight is slow and maneuverable, and they have the ability to hover. Females are generally larger than males.

Primary Threat(s): Habitat Loss, white-nose syndrome (a deadly fungal disease), human interference with roosting sites which leaves to site abandonment. **The Bureau of Land Management (BLM) also lists this bat as a "Sensitive Species".**

Photo by Kristin Szabo (http://heritage.nv.gov/)

Mountain Cottontail Rabbit *(Sylvilagus nuttallii)*

Species is "Secure" at This Time

Primary Habitat: Eight species of Cottontail Rabbits are found in California, and they inhabit brushy or wooded areas on slopes or riverbanks that are often covered with grasses, willows, and most importantly, sagebrush. They can be found throughout the Berryessa Snow Mountain region. If vegetation is sparse, as on a rocky mountainside, these rabbits can hide in burrows or rock crevices. The ears are shorter than those of jackrabbits, and have black tips.

These rabbits usually eat grasses but will also eat fruits and shrubs. Females can have up to five litters a year and each litter can have as many as eight bunnies each. Predation of these rabbits - by raptors, coyotes, and foxes - is high, so they don't live very long.

Mountain Cottontail Rabbit. Photo by Mary K. Hanson.

Primary Threat(s): Invasive rabbit species that compete for food; loss of habitat; intentional killing by humans; pesticide and herbicide use.

Mountain Lion, Cougar *(Puma concolor)*

California Species of Special Concern

Primary Habitat: More than half of California is prime Mountain Lion habitat. Foothills and mountains are most suitable. **Generally speaking, Mountain Lions can be found wherever deer are present since deer are a Mountain Lion's main food source.** (Calif. Dept. of Fish & Wildlife). An estimated 4,000 to 5,000 Mountain Lions inhabit California, and their range frequently putting them in close proximity to humans in foothill and mountain areas. Mountain Lions have the largest range of any wild cat. They have been spotted throughout the Berryessa Snow Mountain region; in fact, many public land areas have signage warning about Mountain Lions. The big cats are most active at dawn and sunset, but also roam during the night.

Photo by Mary K. Hanson

Mountain Lions are solitary animals (except when mating, from December to March) and have wide ranges (from 10 to 35 miles) over which they are highly territorial. Females can have two to four kittens (or cubs) in a litter.

Primary Threat(s): Habitat loss and fragmentation, persecution as a pest animal, poaching (in California, where the lions can only be killed under very specific circumstances), and loss of prey animals. Mountain lions are legally classified as "specially protected species". This does not imply that they are rare. Rather it means that **in California it is "illegal to take, injure, possess, transport, import, or sell any mountain lion or part of a mountain lion."**

For more information see the Mountain Lion Foundation of Sacramento's website at: http://mountainlion.org/index.asp

Mule Deer, Columbia Black-Tailed Mule Deer *(Odocoileus hemionus columbianus)*

Black-Tailed Mule Deer (adult male). Photo by Mary K. Hanson.

Primary Habitat: Mule Deer live in a broad range of habitats – forests, riparian areas and brushlands. They can be found in every county throughout the Berryessa Snow Mountain region. Some large populations can be seen at the Cache Creek Nature Preserve, the Yolo Bypass Wildlife Area, and the Sacramento National Wildlife Refuge.

Species is "Secure" at This Time

One of the most distinct features of the Mule Deer is its big "mule-like" ears. These ears move constantly and independently. In California there are 6 subspecies of Mule Deer including the Columbia Black-Tailed Deer (like the one in the photo) found in northern California. Their sense of smell is so acute that they can sniff out a human a half-mile away, and can smell water as deep as two feet underground.

Primary Threat(s): High predator populations (including feral dogs), competition with grazing livestock (although in some studies have shown that in some areas cattle actually protect the deer from predators), human alteration of habitat (development, farming), poaching and disease, and impacts with motor vehicles.

Pacific Fisher, West Coast Fisher *(Martes pennanti pacifica)*

Federally Endangered Species

Endangered in California

Primary Habitat: The Pacific Fisher is found only in North America, in intermediate to large tree stages of coniferous forests and deciduous/riparian areas with high percent canopy closure. In the Berryessa Snow Mountain region they are found primarily in Lake and Mendocino Counties. There are small populations around Clear Lake in Lake County, for example. Fishers are creatures of the forests, not water, and their favorite foods are small mammals, not fish. Their unusual common name is thought to come from the French word *fichet*, for the pelt of a European polecat.

Like the martens, fishers are members of the weasel family and are adept at attacking porcupines. Although they mate in April, females can delay implantation of the fertilized eggs in the womb until February or March of the following year!

Primary Threat(s): Habitat loss due to forest fragmentation, logging, fire management practices, and other forest management impacts in remote locations.

On June 11, 2015, in response to a petition and lawsuit from the Center for Biological Diversity, the California Department of Fish and Wildlife today recommended state Endangered Species Act protection for the fisher in the southern Sierra Nevada portion of its range.

Public Domain Photo from the United States Forest Service.

Pallid Bat *(Antrozous pallidus)*

Pallid Bat. Public Domain Photos from http://commons.wikimedia.org/

California Species of Special Concern

Primary Habitat: It can occupy a wide variety of habitats including grasslands, shrublands, woodlands, and forests from sea level up through mixed conifer forests. The species is most common in open, dry habitats with rocky areas for roosting. In the Berryessa Snow Mountain region it is found primarily from Del Norte County to northern Mendocino County.

These bats typically will use three different types of roosts: a day roost which can be a warm, horizontal opening such as rock crevices (or in "bat boxes" and attics); the night roost is in the open but with foliage nearby; and a hibernation roost (such as caves). Insects are the mainstay of their diet, and they eat a variety of moths, Jerusalem crickets, grasshoppers, and scorpions. "Leftovers" of these meals are often found on the ground below where the bats roost. Pallid bats have eyes that are larger than any other bat species in the United States. Twin births are very common for these bats.

Primary Threat(s): Loss of habitat; human encroachment into and disturbance of roosting areas, and pesticide use.

River Otter, North American River Otter *(Lontra canadensis)*

Species is "Secure" at This Time

Primary Habitat: River Otters occupy streams, lakes, ponds, swamps, marshes, estuaries, and beaver flowages. They are found throughout most of North America north of Mexico, except the extreme southwestern US. In California, River Otters can be found through most of the state's major river systems and appear in 31 of the state's 58 counties. The most dense concentration of otters is in the Sacramento River delta, but there are also large, healthy populations in the Klamath, Trinity, Eel, Feather and Pit River systems. In the Berryessa Snow Mountain region they can often be found along Cache Creek and Putah Creek and are seasonal visitors to the Yolo Basin, Cache Creek Nature Preserve, Conaway Ranch, and the Sacramento County Bufferlands area.

River Otters are probably best known for their sense of fun. While most mammals play and romp only while they're young, otters are always looking for things to play with and places to slide even throughout their adult years. They play socially as well, and social groups are usually made up of a female and her offspring. Otters don't breed until they are about two years old, and females can delay the implantation of fertilized eggs for almost a year. Birthing usually takes place in April, and there are most often two or three young in a "bevy". Their dens are called "couches".

River Otter primarily eat fish, but in California where fish populations are sometime migratory, the otters will also eat crustaceans, insects, mollusks, crayfish, frogs, rodents and turtles. In some months crayfish will make up 50 to 80% of the otter's diet.

Primary Threat(s): Water pollution and habitat destruction rank among the most serious threats to River Otters.

River Otters on the north shore of Cache Creek. Photo by Bob Schneider.

San Joaquin Pocket Mouse *(Perognathus inornatus)*

Listed by NatureServe as Vulnerable – a species at moderate risk of extinction or elimination due to a restricted range, relatively few populations, recent and widespread declines, or other factors.

Primary Habitat: A California **native**, the San Joaquin Pocket Mouse is found in west-central California. **In Lake County, it occurs on rocky south-facing slope in chamise and buck brush chaparral at elevations around 1300 feet.**

This species inhabits dry, open, grassy or weedy ground, arid annual grasslands, and savanna associated with sandy washes or finely textured soil.

Primary Threat(s): More than 90% of the original habitat has been destroyed as a result of expanding development (NatureServe).

San Joaquin Pocket Mouse. Photo by "Jon" at http://mammalwatching.wordpress.com/

Silver Haired Bat *(Lasionycteris noctivagans)*

Listed by NatureServe as Vulnerable – a species at moderate risk of extinction or elimination due to a restricted range, relatively few populations, recent and widespread declines, or other factors.

Primary Habitat: The distribution of the Silver-Haired Bats includes forests from the Oregon border south. This species has been found in Sacramento, Stanislaus, Monterey and Yolo Counties. Summer habitats include coniferous forests, valley foothill woodlands, pinyon-juniper woodlands, and riparian habitats. *"During spring and fall migrations the silver-haired bat may be found anywhere in California. There may be some sexual segregation in the summer range, females occurring further to the north. Silver-haired bats are common, but erratic in abundance."* [Dept. of Fish and Wildlife]

These bats feed primarily on moths and other soft-bodied insects which they hunt over streams, ponds, and open bushy areas. They require a lot of water and usually roosts and breeds near regions where water is easily accessible. They prefer to roost in tree hollows, buildings, caves, abandoned mines and under bark.

Primary Threat(s): Pesticide use and loss of habitat; the Silver-Haired Bat is one of the three tree bat species most commonly killed at wind energy facilities (over 75% of the mortalities). [Journal of Wildlife Management.72:61–78]

Photo from the Animal Diversity Web.
(It gets its name from the silver-tips on the fur on its back.)

Tule Elk (*Cervus canadensis*)

Tule Elk. Public Domain Photos from http://www.public-domain-image.com/

Species is "Secure" at This Time

Primary Habitat: Over the past several years, this elk has become one of iconic symbols of wildlife within the Berryessa Snow Mountain region. Tule Elk are **endemic to California** and can be found ranging from the grasslands and marshlands of the Central Valley to the grassy hills on the coast. **Tule Elk can be found locally in the Cache Creek Natural Area (usually around Cowboy Camp) and on the Point Reyes National Seashore.** This subspecies of elk found only in California had been hunted and poached so extensively that by 1870 they were actually thought to be extinct. Thanks to conservation efforts, including those by California cattle baron Henry Miller in 1873 (who spared and protected several of the elk on his ranch) and the California Department of Fish and Wildlife, the state population is now over 4000 individuals. They are no longer considered endangered. The herd at Cache Creek did better than most of the herds placed throughout the state in part because it was "relocated" to land that was part of the elk's original territory, and in part because the herd members were relatively young and robust. In the wild, the elk live about 12 years.

During the breeding season in the fall, mature bull elk "in rut" will use their antlers in part to intimidate younger males, but also as weapons against well-matched bulls to establish dominance when less violent alternatives like vocalization (called "bugling") and posturing fail. As his prize for winning, the dominant male gets to do 80% of the breeding in the herd. Mated females will have their calves, weighing in at around 20 pounds at birth, a little more than eight months later, usually in May and June. The youngsters are weaned within a few months, just as their spotted coat is replaced by the traditional "Tule-Elk-Tan" coat, and immediately join the herd.

The Tule Elk are sometimes inaccurately referred to as "dwarf elk" because they are generally smaller in size than other species, like the Rocky Mountain Elk. The smaller size of most Tule Elk is attributed in part to genetics and in part to their diet which consists of a variety of grasses, leaves, reeds and forbs (such as sunflowers and milkweed), and aquatic vegetation when available. Although most male Tule elk (called "bulls") weigh between 450 and 500 pounds, and the females (called "cows") weigh around 350 to 425 pounds, the California Department of Fish and Wildlife records an elk in the Grizzly Island Wildlife Area at Suisun City weighing in at about 900 pounds. Still, even a 500-pound male is a pretty awesome sight. Standing at up to 5 feet high at the shoulder, adult males can be about 7 feet long and sport a rack of heavy 6-point antlers which by themselves can weigh upwards of 40 pounds.

Viewing these creatures can be a lot of fun, but for your own safety and the safety of the elk, follow these basic guidelines: (1) View the elk at a distance. Using the telephoto setting on your camera, a scope, or binoculars are ideal. (2) Never get between a cow and her calf. (3) Never put yourself between a dominant bull and his harem, or any bull and its rival. (4) Whisper, watch quietly, and keep your movements slow. If you come across some antlers that have been shed, leave them where they are. Rodents and deer use them as a source of calcium. When in the wild remember: *take only photographs and memories.*

Primary Threat(s): loss of genetic diversity (caused by "bottlenecking" of herds), invasive plant species in the areas where the elk forage which leads to malnutrition and starvation.

Townsend's Big-Eared Bat *(Corynorhinus townsendii)*

Public Domain Image from Creative Commons

California Species of Special Concern

Federal Species of Special Concern

Primary Habitat: These bats are found throughout California in a wide variety of habitats. Generally viewed as a cave dwelling species, the two western subspecies are also found in human-made structures (e.g. old mine workings and buildings).

Regionally, there are populations in the counties of Del Norte, Mendocino, Sonoma, Lake, Colusa, Yolo, and Napa. Unlike many species which take refuge in crevices, this bat only roosts in the open, hanging from walls and ceilings where it is relatively easily detected and particularly vulnerable to disturbance. They will abandon their roosts if they are disturbed and this adds to their declining populations. Human incursion into the hibernating sites at Bartlett Mountain in Lake County, for example, caused a sharp decline in the bat populations there. The bats will eventually return to roosting sites if they are left undisturbed for a period of time.

The bat's ears are its major feature. When this bat's long ears are laid back, they can reach back to the middle of its body.

Primary Threat(s): loss of habitat; human intrusion into roosting sites; extermination by pest control companies, excessive collection for scientific purposes. **This species of bat is also on the Forest Service "Sensitive species" list, the Bureau of Land Management "Sensitive species" list, and the Western Bat Working Group "High Priority" species list.**

Yuma Myotis Bat (Myotis yumanensis)

Species is "Secure" at This Time

Primary Habitat: This bat lives in a variety of lowland habitats, including riparian, scrublands and forests, but it has a very close association with water.

Yumas tend to feed on insects: moths, beetles, caddis flies, midges, flying ants and termites, mosquitoes, and diptera (true flies). After feeding, they periodically rest at night roosts where the food is digested. The species roosts under bridges, in buildings, cliff crevices, caves, mines, and trees. They mate in the fall, and females give birth between May and June. Females normally give birth to only one pup. Individuals are usually brown or pale tan (like the one in our photo).

Primary Threat(s): Loss of water habitat where their prey insects live. Human interference. According to the Bureau of Land Management: *"Bats live in natural structures like caves, but they also live in manmade structures such as bridges and abandoned mines. Vandalism in these areas drives the bats away and kills many of them."* Conservation efforts include building new bridges and maintaining old bridges where the bats are know to roost, and doing studies for the bat before closing down abandoned mine sites. Although it's not on any state or federal list, **the Bureau of Land Management lists this bat as a "Sensitive Species".**

Yuma Myotis Bat. Photo by J. N. Stuart.

Blue Belly Lizard, Western Fence Lizard *(Sceloporus occidentalis)*

Photo from US Forest Service Pacific Southwest Research Station

Primary Habitat: Found throughout California, the Western Fence Lizard can also be found as far north as Seattle, Washington and as far south as Baja California. They live in a variety of habitats including grasslands, chaparral, sagebrush, woodlands, coniferous forests, riparian areas, and farmlands.

These lizards are regularly seen along hiking trails in the Berryessa Snow Mountain region where they can find quick cover under plants, rocks, and fallen trees.

The behavior most noted by those that come across them is the male lizard's ritual of shimmying, bouncing, and doing "push ups" to impress the females and ward off other encroaching males.

Although the taxonomy of this lizard has been, and still is, under debate, what distinguishes it from similar species such as the Eastern Fence Lizard and the Sagebrush Lizard, are the bright blue patches on its belly and throat and the yellow markings on the legs. Prominent in adult males, these patches are duller or nonexistent in females and juveniles of the species.

Primary Threat(s): Unknown

Species is "Secure" at This Time

California Kingsnake *(Lampropeltis californiae)*

Species is "Secure" at This Time

Primary Habitat: This is a relatively small, non-venomous subspecies of the common kingsnake, and is found in a variety of habitats including foothills, riparian areas, oak forests, coastal scrub areas, grasslands, and chaparral.

Coloring can vary greatly. The one in our photo is black and white, but they can also be gray and white, or brown and white... and there are even some unusual striped morphs. Some kingsnakes can also sport a red-white-and-black banding pattern which causes some people mistake them for poisonous coral snakes. How do you tell them apart? Remember this: *"If red touches yellow, you're a dead fellow, but if red touches black then you're all right Jack."*

The name "king" refers to this snake's propensity to occasionally eat other snakes -- including rattlesnakes. They have a high tolerance to rattlesnake venom, but are not entirely immune.

Primary Threat(s): Unknown.

California Kingsnake versus a Rattlesnake. Public Domain Photo.

California Newt *(Taricha torosa)*

ABOVE: California Newt underwater, photo by Andrew Fulks.
BELOW: Mating newts and egg masses, photo by Gary Nafis and californiaherps.com.

California Species of Special Concern

Primary Habitat: This brightly-colored newt is found **almost exclusively in California**. It breeds in ponds, reservoirs and streams, but during non-breeding seasons it prefers to live in adjacent grasslands, woodlands and forests. It's not uncommon to see large groups of these newts traveling from one habitat to another. The most recent sightings in the local region include the areas along Cache Creek and across the Berryessa Peak Trail. Conservationist, Bob Schneider (one of the founders of Tuleyome), recalls a hike one morning when he encountered over 100 California Newts on the Berryessa Peak Trail moving from one water source to another.

Reproduction occurs between December and May, and eggs are usually laid attached to sticks, stones or vegetation in non-flowing water. "Newts" are salamanders that spend most of their time on land. These newts are reddish on top and golden-yellow underneath. Their skin is rough but not slimy. However, the newts' skin secretes a neurotoxin called tetrodotoxin (like that of the pufferfish). The poison is strong enough to kill a human if it is ingested. Because of this natural toxicity, the newts have few natural predators, although some species of garter snake have developed a resistance to the toxin.

Primary Threat(s): Habitat degradation and loss, increased sedimentation, the introduction of crayfish (which eat the newt's eggs and attack the adults outright) and mosquito fish (which also prey on the eggs of the newts.)

It is illegal to take the newts or their eggs from their environment.

California Red-Legged Frog *(Rana draytonii)*

Photo from the US Fish & Wildlife Service, www.fws.gov/

Federally Threatened

California Species of Special Concern

Primary Habitat: This frog is **endemic to California** and can be found in lowlands and foothills in or near permanent sources of deep water with dense, shrubby, or emergent riparian vegetation. This species has disappeared from over 70% of its normal range. The largest population of the frog has been given protection on a 48-acre stretch of land in Placer County. The frogs can sometimes be found at Lake Berryessa, Lake Solano and Clear Lake.

Primary Threat(s): Threats include climate change, loss of habitat, water management issues, drought, vehicles, road expansion, and competition from and predation by non-native bullfrogs (*Rana catesbiana*).

Also listed as a "Vulnerable Species" on the IUCN Red List.

California Tree Frog, Sierran Treefrog *(Pudacseris sierra)*

Primary Habitat: These **indigenous** frogs can be found in almost every part of Central California, around creeks, seasonal creeks, riparian habitats, as well as rocky canyons and washes where there are permanent pools. **In the Berryessa Snow Mountain region they have been found regularly along Putah and Cache Creeks, in Cold Canyon (especially at the pond on the Frog Pond Trail), Brophy Creek, and other similar areas.**

Species is "Secure" at This Time

All tree frogs in California were once lumped together as one species, but have since been broken out into The Baja California Tree Frog, the Northern Pacific Tree Frog, the California Tree Frog and the Sierran Tree Frog (which is the one most common in our part of California.) The Sierran Tree Frog is also known as the "Sierran Chorus Frog" for its penchant for "singing" to others of its kind. The color can vary by region, and camouflages the frogs to look bright green like leaves, or mottled gray and brown like stones around them. A black or dark brown mask (or eye-stripe) is usually present and conspicuous.

Public Domain Image from wikicommons

These frogs attach their eggs in clumps on twigs or sets the mass loose on the bottom of pools. This species requires shade. (UV-B solar radiation reduces embryo survival.)

Primary Threat(s): Human interference; urbanization of habitat areas; water pollution; climate change.

Clear Lake Hitch *(Lavinia exilicauda chi)*

Adult and Juvenile Clear Lake Hitch. Photo from Fishbio.com

Primary Habitat: **This fish is found only in Clear Lake and associated ponds**, though it spawns in streams flowing into the lake. Clear Lake is a popular recreation spot, and is the largest body of freshwater entirely in California; it is estimated to be 2.5 million years old. Once abundant in the lake, and an important part of the natural and cultural heritage of the region, the Hitch have lost access to all but two of their regular spawning streams. These small fish migrate like salmon but not over such long distances.

Primary Threat(s): Loss of habitat due to water diversion, pumping, drought, and pollution; invasive fish and plant species; human interference.

Threatened in California

Previously a "California Species of Special Concern", in 2014 The California Fish and Wildlife Commission upgraded the Hitch to a "threatened species".

Foothill Yellow-Legged Frog *(Rana boylii)*

Primary Habitat: These frogs live in shady, gravelly or rocky streams with riffle areas, chaparral, open woodland areas and forests close to water in California. Breeding takes place in pools of streams, and eggs are usually attached to gravel or rocks at the water's edge. **Although they can be found along streams, creeks and ponds throughout the Berryessa Snow Mountain region, the most documented populations are in Mendocino County.**

California Species of Special Concern

The frogs may be spotted or mottled or plain red, brown or even gray, but all of the adults have yellow coloration along the underside of the legs (usually up to the abdomen). Unlike other frogs in this genus, Yellow-Legged Frogs don't have eye stripes. A buff pattern appears on the snout and breeding males develop "nuptial pads" on their thumbs. They have rough skin and horizontal pupils.

Primary Threat(s): Stream scouring, invasive plant and animal species, pesticides, water pollution and disturbance of the normal temperature and flow of their breeding grounds. In Trinity County, for example, a dam on the frogs' territory resulted in a 94% drop in the possible areas where the frog can breed.

Foothill Yellow-Legged Frog. Photo from the US Forest Service.
(http://www.fs.fed.us/psw/topics/wildlife/herp/rana_boylii/)

Northwestern Pond Turtle *(Actinemys marmorata)*

Northwestern Pond Turtle. Photo by Roger Jones.

Federal Species of Special Concern

Threatened in California

Primary Habitat: This turtle requires both land and water habitats. It swims and feeds in permanent and seasonal rivers, sloughs, streams, lakes, reservoirs, ponds and irrigation canals; and goes onto land to nest, overwinter and bask. They can be found throughout the Berryessa Snow Mountain region, especially in Yolo and Lake County.

Nesting usually occurs within 200 meters of the water source the turtle uses. These turtles are small to medium-sized; drab dark brown, olive brown, or blackish with a low unkeeled shell. The head and legs usually have a network of black speckling on them, and may also show cream or yellowish coloring.

Primary Threat(s): loss of water habitat due to pollution or human interference; disturbance and predation of nesting sites, road mortality, predation of hatchlings by introduced bullfrogs, and small- and large-mouthed bass; removal of turtles from the environment as "pets", and the release of competitive "pet" turtles, like the Red-Cheeked Slider Turtle, into the areas where the pond turtles live and breed. Pesticides and herbicides are also factors in the decline of this turtle.

Pacific Salmon, Chinook Salmon *(Oncorhynchus tshawytscha)*

Primary Habitat: According to the National Oceanic and Atmospheric Administration (NOAA): "Two distinct types or races among Chinook salmon have evolved. One race, described as a 'stream-type' Chinook, is found most commonly in headwater streams of large river systems. The second race, called the 'ocean-type' Chinook, is commonly found in coastal streams. Ocean-type Chinook typically migrate to sea within the first three months of life, but they may spend up to a year in freshwater prior to emigration to the sea."

Federally Endangered Species

Endangered in California

Photo from Fishbio.com. Used for educational purposes.

Salmon can be seen spawning along the Sacramento, American and Feather Rivers and their tributaries in the late fall and early winter. In Yolo County the Yolo Bypass Wildlife Area and several private farms often allow young salmon to feed and grow in flooded rice fields before heading out to the ocean through local waterways.

Primary Threat(s): Water pollution, climate change, variances in water temperatures beyond what the trout can withstand, and habitat loss due to dams, diversions and development are the greatest threats to these fish.

Rainbow Trout, "Steelhead" *(Oncorhynchus mykiss)*

Rainbow Trout / Steelhead. Photo by Mary K. Hanson.

Primary Habitat: These trout occupy fresh, brackish, or marine waters and prefer cool temperatures. Steelhead can be found in streams and rivers throughout northern California including the Eel River, the Sacramento River and the American River. **In 2014 Putah Creek and Lake Solano received "wild trout waters" designations for the populations there.**

Federally Endangered Species

Federally Threatened

Streams must have a mixture of good riffles and pools, shade, and gravel beds where the fish lay their eggs. Steelhead spawn and complete their early development in inland waterways and then spend their adult life at sea before returning to their birthplaces to spawn. Unlike Salmon they do not die after spawning, and can breed for several seasons.

Primary Threat(s): Water pollution, climate change, variances in water temperatures beyond what the trout can withstand, and habitat loss due to dams, diversions and development are the greatest threats to these fish.

Populations in Southern California are considered "Endangered".
Populations in Northern California and the Central Valley are considered "Threatened".

Red Swamp Crawfish *(Procambarus clarkia)*

Species is "Secure" at This Time

Primary Habitat: This species has been introduced throughout the United States, and is able to tolerate a wide range of environmental conditions including high temperatures and low oxygen levels. It can be found in seasonal swamps and marshes, along riparian areas, permanent lakes and streams, wet meadows, culverts and irrigation canals, rice paddy fields, and reservoirs. In Yolo County they can also be found in rice fields, urban ponds and other areas that provide them with a ready supply of water.

It is a major commercial crayfish and is also **highly invasive**.

These crawfish (or "crayfish") build smokestack-like structures out of mud, called "chimneys" that are open on the top to allow for air flow but are full of water at the bottom. Each chimney houses a single crawfish. Where chimney-building isn't feasible, the crawfish will burrow into the ground during the molting season. Where crawfish populations are dense, this burrowing sometimes causes damage to levees and other earthen water-control structures. Another problem is this species' diet. Most crawfish eat plants, but this one eats insects, snails, larvae and eggs. **Since its introduction into California this adaptable and aggressive crawfish has become a major threat to some native species -- such as the California Newt.** It is also known to carry parasitic worms that can create problems for native animals.

Primary Threat(s): Unknown.

Photo by Mary K. Hanson.

Sacramento Perch *(Archoplites interruptus)*

California Species of Special Concern

Primary Habitat: Sacramento Perch are the **only surviving native** species of Sunfish (*centrarchid*) in California. Native Americans in the region historically depended on the perch as a main part of their diet. The fish live in rivers, lakes and sloughs, and **there is a small but persistent population of them in Clear Lake in Lake County.**

Adult perch have brown bodies with dark vertical stripes and a black spot on the "ear" flap behind the eye. They grow to be about 2 ½ feet long. The perch were reintroduced in many other states, but they don't transplant well. Only those in Nevada and Utah still exist.

Juvenile Sacramento Perch. Photo from UC Davis's "California Fish Species" website.. Used for educational purposes.

Primary Threat(s): Loss of habitat, manipulation of habitat by humans and the introduction of non-native fish (especially the Bluegill and Black Crappie) that eat the perch's' eggs and compete with them for food and breeding sights. Agricultural runoff and water pollution are also factors.

This fish is also listed as an "Endangered Species" on the International Union for Conservation of Nature (IUCN) Red List. It is also listed as "Threatened" by the American Fisheries Society.

Western Rattlesnake => Northern Pacific Rattlesnake *(Crotalus oreganus)*

Primary Habitat: These snakes occupy a wide range of habitats including coastal dunes, timberlines, riparian areas, shrubby basins, chaparral, canyons and mountain forests. When inactive it occupies secluded sites like caves, burrows and crevices. Pregnant females often congregate in a winter den until they give birth. **Rattlesnakes are prevalent throughout the Berryessa Snow Mountain region, and have been photographed along many of the hiking trails and on Tuleyome's Goat Mountain property.**

Species is "Secure" at This Time

At one time, all Western Rattlesnakes were classified under *Crotalus viridis*, but they have since been split up, and the one most prominent in northern California is now called *Crotalus oreganus* or the Northern Pacific Rattlesnake.

Unlike many snakes, rattlesnake females are "ovoviviparous", which means they carry their eggs inside their bodies and then give birth to live young.

Primary Threat(s): Habitat loss, persecution and deliberate killing by humans, development and urbanization. Some snakes are also killed by motor vehicles.

Northern Pacific Rattlesnake. Photo by Sam Murray.

FLORA

- Flowers, Plants & Grasses
- Trees
- Fungus & Lichen
- Common Slime Molds

Flowers and Plants Listed by Color

All of the flowers, plants and grasses in this guide are listed in alphabetical order, but to help you locate a specific flower we have also listed them by color here. You may find some flowers listed under more than one color. This is because the flowers may be found in a variety of different colors/tints throughout the Berryessa Snow Mountain region, or their blossoms have more than one predominant color.

Blue
- Baby Blue Eyes
- Bird's Eyes
- Blue Dicks
- Few-Flowered Navarretia (*white or pale blue*)
- Holly-Leaf Ceanothus
- Many-Flowered Navarretia
- Rincon Ridge Ceanothus
- Western Larkspur (*can be dark blue, pink or white*)

Green
- Brittlescale
- Eelgrass / Pond Weed
- Green Jewel Flower, Serpentine Jewel-flower
- Pipevine, California Pipevine
- Porcupine Sedge
- San Joaquin Spearscale
- Scalloped Moonwort
- Slender Orcutt Grass
- Stoney Creek Spurge
- Tule

Orange
- California Poppy
- Paintbrush, Indian Paintbrush
- Narrowleaf Milkweed (*blossoms can be pink or orange*)

Pink (or Deep Pink)
- Adobe Lily
- Balloon Clover
- Cob Mountain Lupine
- Drymaria-Like Western Flax (*pink stripes on white petals*)
- Indian Valley Brodiaea
- Jepson's Baby Stars
- Marsh Checkerbloom
- Most Beautiful Jewel Flower
- Narrowleaf Milkweed (*blossoms can be pink or orange*)
- Pink Creamsacs, Creamsacs
- Red Flowered Bird's-Foot Trefoil
- Red Mountain Catchfly
- Shooting Star, "Mosquito Bill"
- Showy Milkweed
- Snow Mountain Buckwheat
- Snow Mountain Willowherb
- Sonoma Beardtongue, Mountain Pride
- Twining Lily
- Western Larkspur (*can be blue, pink or white*)

Purple (or Lavender)
- Bird's Eyes
- Buckbrush, Wedgeleaf Ceanothus (*sometimes have a purple tint*)
- Freed's Jewel Flower
- Jepson's Milk Vetch
- Jimson Weed (*can be white, cream or purple*)
- Narrow Anthered California Brodiaea
- Rincon Ridge Ceanothus

- Robust Monardella, Coyote Mint

Red (or Maroon, Deep Red)
- Indian Warrior
- Paintbrush, Indian Paintbrush
- Red Flowered Bird's-Foot Trefoil
- Scarlet Larkspur
- Shooting Star, "Mosquito Bill"
- Slender Orcutt Grass
- Sonoma Beardtongue, Mountain Pride

White (or Cream)
- Anthony Peak Lupine
- Baker's Navarretia
- Bogg's Lake Hedge Hyssop
- Bolander's Horkelia
- Brandegee's Eriastrum
- Buckbrush, Wedgeleaf Ceanothus
- Coastal Bluff Morning Glory
- Coyote Brush
- Drymaria-Like Western Flax
- Dwarf Downingia
- Dwarf Soaproot
- Few-Flowered Navarretia *(white or pale blue)*
- Jimson Weed *(can be white, cream or purple)*
- Legenere
- Manroot, California Manroot, "Big Root"
- Marin County Navarretia
- Morrison's Jewel Flower
- Pink Creamsacs, Creamsacs
- Red Mountain Catchfly
- Round-Leaf Stork's Bill, Large-Leaved Filaree
- Sambucas, Blue Elderberry
- Serpentine Cryptantha
- Western Larkspur *(can be dark blue, pink or white)*

Yellow
- Bare Monkey Flower
- Bent-Flowered Fiddleneck
- Big-Scale Balszmroot
- Brewer's Western Flax
- Burke's Goldfields
- California Poppy
- Colusa Layai
- Contra Costa Goldfields
- Glandular Dwarf Flax
- Gold Nugget, Yellow Mariposa Lily
- Golden Fairy Lantern, Diogenes Lantern
- Lake County Stonecrop
- Milo Baker's Lupine
- Morrison's Jewel Flower
- Mount Saint Helen Morning Glory
- Mule Ears
- Napa Western Flax
- Parry's Tarplant
  Small-Flowered Calycandenia
- Tidytips, Common Tidytips *(yellow with white tips)*
- Two-Carpellate Western Flax

Jimson Weed blossom. Photo by Mary K. Hanson

Adobe Lily *(Fritillaria pluriflora)*
Photo by Stacey Flowerdew

Listed as Endangered by the California Native Plant Society (list B1.2)

Primary Habitat: **Endemic to California**, this bulbiferous herb is found in chaparral, cismontane woodland, and valley and foothill grasslands, often in adobe soils.

Primary Threat(s): Grazing, vehicles, development, mining, non-native plants, and horticultural collecting.

Anthony Peak Lupine *(Lupinus antoninus)*
Photo by Rick York and the California Native Plant Society

Listed as Endangered by the California Native Plant Society (list B1.3)

Primary Habitat: **Native**, rare species. **Endemic to California**, this perennial herb is found in lower and upper montane coniferous forests, and prefers rocky soils.

Primary Threat(s): Possibly threatened by hybridization with silver lupine (*Lupinus albifrons var. collinus*)

Baby Blue Eyes *(Nemophila menziesii)*
Photo from westernwildflowers.com

Primary Habitat: An annual herb **native to California** this plant grows virtually all over the state and has even survived introduction in Alaska. It's a major flowering plant for pollinators, and blooms in the spring. It grows in meadows, graslands, chaparral, woodlands, slopes, and along the coast.

Primary Threat(s): Unknown.

Baker's Navarretia
(Navarretia leucocephala ssp. *bakeri)*
Public Domain Photo from Creative Commons and Vernon Smith

Listed as Endangered by the California Native Plant Society (list B1.1)

Primary Habitat: Native rare species. **Endemic to California**, this annual herb is found in vernal pool habitat in cismontane woodlands, lower montane coniferous forests, meadows, seeps, valley and foothill grasslands, and prefers mesic soils.

Primary Threat(s): Expanding development, habitat alteration, road construction, and agriculture.

Balloon Clover *(Trifolium depauperatum)*
Photo from westernwildflowers.com

Listed as S2: Imperiled in California by the California Native Plant Society.

Primary Habitat: A **native** herb, this little plant grows in a variety of habitats and is often found around vernal pools, near marshes and swamps, and alongside other wildflowers in fields throughout northern California. It's also called "Cowsack Clover" or "Poverty Clover". It blooms between February and May.

Primary Threat(s): loss of habitat, development, herbicide use.

Bare Monkey Flower *(Mimulus nudatus)*
Photo by JoAnn Ordano and the California Academy of Sciences.

Listed as Vulnerable by the California Native Plant Society

Primary Habitat: This rare annual herb is **endemic to California** and is found in Lake, Mendocino and Napa Counties. It grows in serpentine seeps, chaparral and cismontane woodland areas, and blooms in a brief period between May and June. The flowers are tube-shaped, bright yellow and have a "pouty lip" with red speckling.

Primary Threat(s): loss of habitat

Bent-Flowered Fiddleneck *(Amsinckia lunaris)*
Public Domain Photo from Creative Commons & Vernon Smith

Listed as Endangered by the California Native Plant Society (list B1.2)

Primary Habitat: **Endemic to central California**, this uncommon fiddleneck grows in the Bay Area and the woods and grasslands of the coastal and inner-coastal mountains and valleys.

Primary Threat(s): Development and Mining

Big-Scale Balszmroot
(Balsamorhiza macrolepis var. *macrolepis)*
Public Domain Photo from Creative Commons and Zoya Akulova

Listed as Endangered by the California Native Plant Society (list B1.2)

Primary Habitat: This **endemic** perennial herb is found in chaparral, inner coastal woodlands, valley and foothill grasslands, and is sometimes found in serpentine soils throughout central California.

Primary Threats: Over-grazing, herbicide use

Bird's Eyes *(Gilia tricolor)*
Public Domain Photo from http://commons.wikimedia.org/

Primary Habitat: This flowering plant is **native to the Central Valley** of California and the foothill areas of the Coast Ranges. Powdery blue stamens set off the pale blue/violet flowers. It's a flower that easy to grow in your backyard native plants garden, and provides nectar and pollen to pollinators of all kinds. This flower has a slightly musky fragrance.

Primary Threat(s): Unknown.

Blue Dicks *(Dichelostemma capitatum)*
Photo by Mary K. Hanson

Primary Habitat: This plant can be found around vernal pools, in woodlands, on hillsides, in grasslands, scrub and coniferous forests, and the flowers bloom between March and May. They rise from a corm (bulbous underground stem base, like a bulb). The corms can sit dormant for over 10 years while they wait for wildfires or other nutrient-rich environmental conditions to trigger blooming. After fires, the plants can bloom vigorously and are drought resistant. The corms are a food source for many local animal species including mule deer, black bears and rabbits.

Primary Threat(s): Unknown

Bogg's Lake Hedge Hyssop *(Gratiola heterosepala)*
Public Domain Photo from Creative Commons and Doug Wirtz.

The California Native Plant Society has considered it to be rare for many years, and currently includes it on its List 1B, noting that it is endangered in a portion of its range. It has, however, been removed from State and Federal listing according to the US Fish and Wildlife Service.

Primary Habitat: This annual herb is a **native** and is found in vernal pool habitats, in marshes and swamps at lake margins. It prefers clay soils, and is most often seen in Lake, Solano, Colusa and Sacramento Counties.

Primary Threat(s): Agriculture, development, grazing, trampling, and vehicles

Bolander's Horkelia *(Horkelia bolanderi)*
Public Domain Photo from Creative Commons and Barry Rice.

Listed as Endangered by the California Native Plant Society (list B1.2)

Primary Habitat: **Endemic to California**, this perennial herb is found in chaparral, lower montane coniferous forest, meadows, seeps, and valley and foothill grasslands, preferring edges and vernally mesic areas.

Primary Threat(s): Vehicles and expanding development

Brandegee's Eriastrum
(Eriastrum brandegeeae)
Public Domain Photo from Creative Commons, Dr. Dean Wm. Taylor.

Listed as Endangered by the California Native Plant Society (list B1.2)

Primary Habitat: **Endemic to California**, this annual herb is found in chaparral and cismontane woodlands, and prefers volcanic and sandy soils. The most reliable occurrence of this rare plant is in Borax Lake, an archaeological site near Clearlake, California.

Primary Threat(s): Grazing, competition, vehicles, recreation, development, and road maintenance (according to the US Dept. of Fish and Wildlife).

Brewer's Western Flax *(Hesperolinon breweri)*
Public Domain Photo from Creative Commons, Dr. Dean Wm. Taylor.

Status – Listed as Endangered by the California Native Plant Society (list B1.2)

The Bureau of Land Management also lists it as a "Sensitive Species"

Primary Habitat: **Endemic to California**, this annual herb is found in chaparral, cismontane woodland, and valley and foothill grasslands, usually in serpentine soils.

Primary Threat(s): Expanding development.

Brittlescale *(Atriplex depressa)*
Public Domain Photo from Creative Commons and Zoya Akulova

Status – Listed as Endangered by the California Native Plant Society (list B1.2)

Primary Habitat: **Endemic to central California**, this annual herb is found among other chenopod shrubs in meadows, playas, alkali sinks,
valley and foothill grasslands, and often near vernal pools in alkaline and clay soils.

Primary Threats: Development, grazing, and trampling

Buckbrush, Wedgeleaf Ceanothus
(Ceanothus cuneatus) Photo from westernwildflower.com

Primary Habitat: It can be found in a variety of habitats but mostly in chaparral and is frequently seen in the coastal ranges. According to the USDA: *"As one of the dominant species in the chaparral ecosystem, this shrub has been utilized by California Native Americans for centuries."* The flowers are white (sometimes with a purple or lavender tint) and the fruit is a round horned capsule that "explodes" to release shiny dark seeds. The explosions are so strong they can catapult the seeds 35 feet into the air and along the ground. Harvester Ants sometimes cache these seeds.

Primary Threat(s): None known

Federally Endangered Species   **Endangered in California**

Burke's Goldfields *(Lasthenia burkei)*
Photo by Rick York and the California Native Plant Society

Primary Habitat: **Endemic to California**, this annual herb is found in vernal pool habitat in mesic meadows and seeps.

Primary Threat(s): Agriculture, urbanization, development, and grazing

California Poppy *(Eschscholzia californica)*
Photo by Mary K. Hanson

Primary Habitat: California poppy was proclaimed the official state flower of California in 1903. A deep-rooted perennial, it is **native to the state**. It can grow along coastal dunes, in redwood forests, valleys, and plains. In the Sacramento Valley, flowering is between March and October. The plants produce long cylindrical seed pods that "explode" and eject the seeds up to 6 feet from the plant. According to the USDA: *"The California poppy has cultural significance for many indigenous people of the western United States including the Luiseno, Cahuilla, Costanoan and Pomo tribes."* Seeds are used in erosion control mixtures, roadside plantings and in restoration projects throughout the state.

Primary Threat(s): Removal of plants by humans (the plants are toxic to livestock)

Coast Range False Bindweed, 3-Fingered Morning Glory *(Calystegia collina* ssp. *tridactylosa)* Public Domain Photo from Creative Commons

Listed as Endangered by the California Native Plant Society (list B1.2)

Primary Habitat: This rhizomatous herb is found in chaparral and cismontane woodlands, as well as in rocky, gravelly openings in the northern inner coastal range.

Primary Threat(s): Expanding development

Coastal Bluff Morning Glory *(Calystegia purpurata* ssp. *saxicola)*
Public Domain Photo from Creative Commons

Listed as Endangered by the California Native Plant Society (list B1.2)

Primary Habitat: This perennial herb is found primarily in coastal dunes and scrub along the central coast, but can also be found in North Coast coniferous forests.

Primary Threat(s): Expanding development, foot traffic, and competition with non-native plants

Cob Mountain Lupine *(Lupinus sericatus)*
Photo from westernwildflowers.com

Listed as Endangered by the California Native Plant Society (list B1.2)

Primary Habitat: **Endemic to California**, this perennial herb is found in broad-leafed upland forests, woodlands, chaparral, cismontane woodlands, and lower montane coniferous forests. Mostly found in the North Coastal Range north of San Francisco.

Primary Threat(s): Geothermal development, habitat alteration, logging, road maintenance and widening, and herbicide application (according to the California Native Plant Society)

Colusa Layai *(Layia septentrionalis)*
Photo from Aaron Arthur and the California Native Plant Society

Listed as Endangered by the California Native Plant Society (list B1.2)

Primary Habitat: **Endemic to California,** this annual herb is found in chaparral, cismontane woodland, and valley and foothill grasslands, and prefers sandy and serpentine soils. **It is only found in 9 counties in California, including Mendocino County.**

Primary Threat(s): Expanding development .

Federally Endangered Species

Contra Costa Goldfields *(Lasthenia conjugens)*
Public Domain Photo from Creative Commons, by Zoya Akulova.

Primary Habitat: **Endemic to California**, this annual herb is found in vernal pool habitat in cismontane woodlands, alkaline playas, and valley and foothill grasslands especially in Napa, Solano, and Sacramento Counties.

Primary Threat(s): Development, habitat alteration, hydrological alterations, overgrazing, competition with non-native plants.

Coyote Brush *(Baccharis pilularis)*
Female flowers (left) and male flowers (right).
Photos from http://www.westernwildflower.com/.

Primary Habitat: Coyote Brush can thrive in a variety of habitats including riparian areas, chaparral, grasslands, foothill woodlands, and closed-cone and mixed-evergreen forests. It is a **native** evergreen shrub that can grow upright or prostrate along the ground and is fairly fire resistant. It's sometimes been used throughout the state for erosion-control, and provides cover to a variety of animals including rabbits and other small mammals. The plants produce male and female flowers that are distinctly different from one another.

Primary Threat(s): Drought, water pollution, diversion of water sources.

This plant is so rare, we don't have a current photo of it!

Dimorphic Snapdragon
(Antirrhinum subcordatum)

Listed as Endangered by the California Native Plant Society (list 4.3)

Primary Habitat: This annual herb is **native to California**, and is found in serpentine chaparral soils, and often near Yellow Pine forests. It usually blooms from April through July.

Primary Threat(s): Logging and development

Drymaria-Like Western Flax
(Hesperolinon drymarioides)
Photo from Niall McCarten and the California Native Plant Society

Listed as Endangered by the California Native Plant Society (list B1.2)

Primary Habitat: **Endemic to California**, this annual herb is found in closed-cone coniferous forests, chaparral, cismontane woodland, and valley and foothill grasslands, and prefers serpentine soils.

Primary Threat(s): Mining and vehicles

Dwarf Downingia *(Downingia pusilla)*
Public Domain Photo from Creative Commons, Dr. Dean Wm. Taylor.

Listed as Endangered by the California Native Plant Society (list 2.2)
Listed as S2—Imperiled by the State of California.

Primary Habitat: This annual herb is found in vernal pool habitat in valley and foothill grasslands. The tiny blossoms appear between March and May.

Primary Threat(s): Urbanization, development, agriculture, non-native plants, and industrial forestry (according to the California Native Plant Society). Individual populations may also be threatened by off-road recreational vehicles and overgrazing.

Dwarf Soaproot
(Chlorogalum pomeridianum var. *minus)*
Public Domain Photo from Creative Commons, Dr. Dean Wm. Taylor.

Listed as Endangered by the California Native Plant Society (list B1.2)

Primary Habitat: **Endemic to California**, this native perennial herb prefers chaparral in serpentine soils, but it can also be found in grasslands, and pine– and hardwood forests. Plants can regenerate from seed or from their underground bulbs (which are sometimes activated by wildfires).

Primary Threat(s): Unknown, but might be affected by overgrazing.

Eelgrass / Pond Weed
(Potamogeton zosteriformis)
Photo by Donald Cameron at https://gobotany

Listed as Endangered by the California Native Plant Society (list 2.2)

Primary Habitat: **Native to California.** This aquatic herb is found in freshwater marshes and swamps, wetlands, and riparian habitats throughout the Central Valley. It blooms in June and July. Locally it can be found in Lake and Sacramento Counties.

Primary Threat(s): Habitat destruction, water pollution, water diversion.

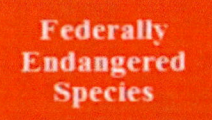 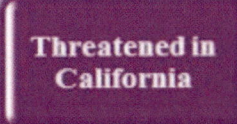

Few-Flowered Navarretia
(Navarretia leucocephala ssp. *pauciflora)*
Photo by Jake Ruygt from the CA Department of Fish and Wildlife

Primary Habitat: **Endemic to California**, this annual herb is found in vernal pools and prefers volcanic ash flow. It forms mats that produce up to 20 flower heads of white or pale blue flowers. It's so rare that there are only eight documented populations in the state; one is at Mead Ranch, which is protected from development by a conservation easement held by the Napa Valley Land Trust.

Primary Threat(s): development, ground water contamination and runoff.

Freed's Jewel Flower
(Streptanthus brachiatus ssp. hoffmannii)
Photo by Sangeet Khalsa and CalPhotos

Listed as Endangered by the California Native Plant Society (list B1.2)

Primary Habitat: **Endemic to California**, this perennial herb is found in chaparral and cismontane woodlands, and prefers serpentine soils.

Primary Threat(s): Urbanization and expanding development

Glandular Dwarf Flax
(Hesperolinon adenophyllum)
Photo by John Game and CalPhotos

Listed as Endangered by the California Native Plant Society (list B1.2)

Primary Habitat: **Endemic to California,** this annual herb is found in chaparral, cismontane woodlands, and valley and foothill grasslands, and prefers serpentine soils.

Primary Threat(s): Geothermal development, recreation, and grazing.

Gold Nugget, Yellow Mariposa Lily
(Calochortus luteus) Photo by Mary K. Hanson

Primary Habitat: This lily is **endemic to California,** and can be found in grasslands, coastal prairies, woodlands, and mix-evergreen forests and on open forest floors. Local populations can be found Yolo and Sacramento Counties and throughout central western California. The southern Paiute and Sierra Miwok Indians used to gather the bulbs for food with digging sticks. The bulbs are now often used in landscape design as ornamental plants and are also used in some restoration projects.

Primary Threat(s): Development, herbicide use

Golden Fairy Lantern, Diogenes Lantern
(Calochortus amabilis) Photo by Mary K. Hanson

Primary Habitat: This lily is **endemic to northern California**, and prefers foothill woodlands, oak woodlands, chaparral and mixed-evergreen forests. It can be found throughout Yolo, Lake, and Solano Counties. It blooms from April until June. The stems are flat and waxy and each bears one or two "heavily nodding" globe-like flowers that are golden yellow. Flowers are later replaced by lobed seed pods. (This photo was taken in the Highland Springs area in Lake County.)

Primary Threat(s): Development, herbicide use

Green Jewel Flower, Serpentine Jewelflower
(Streptanthus hesperidis)
Public Domain Photo from Creative Commons. Dr. Dean Wm. Taylor.

Listed as Endangered by the California Native Plant Society (list B1.2)

Primary Habitat: **Endemic to California**, this annual herb is found in open chaparral and cismontane woodlands, and prefers serpentine and rocky soils. It blooms from May through July and is favored by the California Marble butterfly. It's found mostly in Lake and Napa County, but smaller populations exist in Glenn and Colusa County.

Primary Threat(s): loss of habitat, mining

Holly-Leaf Ceanothus *(Ceanothus purpureus)*
Photo from westernwildflowers.com

Listed as Endangered by the California Native Plant Society (list B1.2)

Primary Habitat: **Endemic to California**, this evergreen shrub is found in chaparral and cismontane woodland, and prefers volcanic and rocky soils. It's found mostly in Napa County, but can also be found in Solano and Mendocino Counties.

Primary Threat(s): Loss of habitat due to agricultural and residential development, and alteration of fire regimes.

Endangered in California

Indian Valley Brodiaea *(Brodiaea rosea)*
Photo by Rick York and the California Native Plant Society

Primary Habitat: **Endemic to California**, this bulbiferous herb is found in the inner coastal range in closed-cone coniferous forest, chaparral, cismontane woodland, and valley and foothill grasslands, often in serpentine soils.

Primary Threats: Vehicles, dumping, and horticultural collecting

Indian Warrior *(Pedicularis densiflora)*
Photo by Mary K. Hanson

Primary Habitat: This **California native** can be found in foothills, oak woodlands, forest and chaparral throughout the state. Large populations exist in Lake, Mendocino and Napa County, but some smaller populations have also been noted in Yolo and Solona County. It's a perennial herb that is root-parasitic. Although it can live by itself, it will attach itself to the roots of other plants (especially manzanita) to obtain water and nutrients. It has green, red or magenta stems and sprouts long spikes of red to bright pink flowers with "toothy" petals.

Primary Threat(s): Unknown.

Jepson's Baby Stars *(Leptosiphon jepsonii)*
Photo from westernwildflowers.com

Listed as Endangered by the California Native Plant Society (list B1.2)
Listed as S2 Imperiled by the State of California.

Primary Habitat: **Endemic to California**, this annual herb is found in broad-leafed upland forests and cismontane woodlands in northwestern California. It generally blooms from March through May. The largest populations are in Napa County, but smaller populations have been found in Yolo and Lake County as well.

Primary Threat(s): Expanding development

Jepson's Milk Vetch
(Astragalus rattanii var. jepsonianus)
Public Domain Photo from Creative Commons, Vernon Smith.

Listed as Endangered by the California Native Plant Society (list B1.2)

Primary Habitat: An annual herb **endemic to California**, Jepson's Milk Vetch occurs in chaparral, valley and foothill grasslands, and serpentine soils in the inner coastal range.

Primary Threats: Development and habitat destruction

Jimson Weed (*Datura stramonium*)
Photo by Mary K. Hanson

Primary Habitat: It's **native** to North America but can now be found all over the world. A member of the deadly nightshade family, this large-leaved plant blooms throughout the summer with long trumpet-like flowers that can be white, cream or purple. When the flowers die they are replaced by large globe-shaped seed pods covered with spines. Each pod contains dozens of seed that are belched out when the pods break open. The plant has hallucinogenic properties, but because the oxtropane alkaloids that produces the effect are also highly toxic, use can easily result in hospitalization or death.

Primary Threat(s): Unknown.

Federally Endangered Species **Endangered in California**

Lake County Stonecrop *(Sedella leiocarpa)*
Photo by Cherilyn Burton and CalPhotos.

Primary Habitat: **Endemic to California**, this annual herb is found in cismontane woodland, valley and foothill grasslands, and vernally mesic depressions in volcanic outcrops.

Primary Threat(s): Extremely vulnerable to trampling; grazing, altered hydrology, and development

This plant is so rare, we don't have a current photo of it!

Lake County Western Flax
(Hesperolinon didymocarpum)

Primary Habitat: **Endemic to California**, this annual herb is found in chaparral, cismontane woodland, and valley and foothill grasslands, and prefers serpentine soils.

Primary Threat(s): Grazing, agriculture, and urbanization

Legenere *(Legenere limosa)*
Photo by John Game

Listed as Endangered by the California Native Plant Society (list B1.1)

Primary Habitat: **Endemic to California**, this annual herb is found in vernal pools. It is found mainly in Sacramento and Solano Counties, but is has also been reported in 12 other north-central and bay-delta counties. While Legenere has not been found in the Natomas Basin, vernal pool habitat exists on the eastern edge of the basin, north of Del Paso Road.

Primary Threat(s): loss of habitat, drought, grazing, road widening, non-native plants, and development.

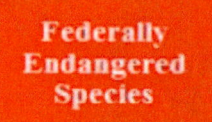

Many-Flowered Navarretia
(Navarretia leucocephala ssp. *plieantha)*
Public Domain Photo from Creative Commons, by Don Loarie.

Primary Habitat: **Endemic to California**, this annual herb is found in vernal pools in the inner coastal range.

Primary Threat(s): Loss of habitat, climate change, drought, grazing, development, water pollution.

Manroot, California Manroot, "Big Root" *(Marah fabaceus)*
Photos by Mary K. Hanson

Primary Habitat: Often mistaken for wild grapevines, the California Manroot (or Bigroot) is the largest and most common manroot **native to California**. This plant can be found throughout the state in a variety of habitats. Hybrid versions are also very common. They are vaguely related to cucumbers but are not edible.

These vines thrive in riparian habitat, beside streams, creeks or washes, but they have also been found in chaparral. The vines can grow in a variety of soils, but need moist ground. The vines are thick, hearty and "hairy" and can climb or race to a length of about 20 feet. Both male and female flowers grow on the same plant. Males appear in clusters, and females (with a bulb-like base) appear individually. The vines usually sprout in the spring, fruit, and then die out in the heat of summer.

The underground tuberous "big root" that supports the plant can weigh as much as 200 pounds.

The "fruit", a large seed pod, is round and covered with soft spines. Usually the size of a golf ball, they can grow as large as oranges if left undisturbed. The pods are green to start with and then turn yellow-brown before breaking open at the bottom to let loose 3 or 4 very large pale seeds. The fruit is not edible and can induce vomiting and diarrhea.

Primary Threat(s): Climate change, drought, loss of habitat, destruction or removal of vines by humans, development.

Marin County Navarretia
(Navarretia rosulata)
Public Domain Photo from Creative Commons

Listed as Endangered by the California Native Plant Society (list B1.2)

Primary Habitat: **Endemic to California**, this annual herb is found in closed-cone coniferous forests and chaparral, and prefers serpentine and rocky soils. As its name implies it's found in Marin County, but populations have also been noted in Napa County.

Primary Threat(s): loss of habitat, expanding development

Marsh Checkerbloom
(Sidalcea oregana ssp. hydrophila)
Photo by Jennifer L. Kalt and CalPhotos.

Listed as Endangered by the California Native Plant Society (list B1.2)

Primary Habitat: **Endemic to California**, this perennial herb is found in meadows, seeps, and riparian forests throughout the central valley.

Primary Threat(s): loss of habitat,, drought, expanding development

Threatened in California

Milo Baker's Lupine *(Lupinus milo-bakeri)*
Public Domain Photo by John Rusk.

Primary Habitat: **Endemic to California**, this annual herb is found in cismontane woodlands, valley and foothill grasses, and often along roadsides. It's found primarily in Colusa and Mendocino County. It blooms from June to September. This plant highly toxic and is listed as "Major" on the California Poison Control list.

Primary Threat(s): Urbanization, road widening, and herbicide application.

Morrison's Jewel Flower
(Streptanthus morrisonii ssp. morrisonii)
Public Domain Photo from Creative Commons, Vernon Smith

Listed as Endangered by the California Native Plant Society (list B1.2)

Primary Habitat: **Endemic to California**, this perennial herb is found in chaparral in serpentine or rocky soil. It's mostly found in Sonoma County, but populations have also been noted in Lake, Napa, Colusa and Glenn Counties. Hard calyxes grow from the stem and the petals emerging from them are white with purple-brown veins.

Primary Threat(s): loss of habitat, expanding development

Most Beautiful Jewel Flower
(Streptanthus albidus ssp. peramoenus)
Photo by Robert Sikora and CalPhotos

Listed as Endangered by the California Native Plant Society (list B1.2)

Primary Habitat: This gem-colored annual herb is **endemic to California** and blooms from April to September in foothill woodlands, chaparral, and valley grasslands. In the local region it's found mostly in Lake and Napa County, but small populations have also been noted in Yolo and other counties throughout the state.

Primary Threat(s): Development, competition with non-native plants and over-grazing.

Mount Saint Helen Morning Glory
(Calystegia collina ssp. oxyphylla)
Photo from westernwildflowers.com

Listed as Endangered by the California Native Plant Society (list 4.2)

Primary Habitat: **Endemic to California**, this rhizomatous herb (a member of the morning glory family) is found in chaparral, lower montane coniferous forest, and valley and foothill grasslands, primarily in the northern central inner-coastal range. It's often found in serpentine soils. Locally it can be found in Lake, Napa and Colusa Counties,

Primary Threat(s): development, road maintenance

Mule Ears *(Wyethia glabra)*
Photo by Mary K. Hanson

Primary Habitat: This plant is part of the Aster family, is **endemic to California**, and grows in grasslands, chaparral and mixed-evergreen forest area, as well as foothills. It blooms from March to May. It gets its name from the long lance-shaped oval leaves that surround the plant's single flower. Locally it can be found in Lake, Napa and Mendocino Counties.

The photo to the right shows one growing in the Highland Springs area of Lake County.

Primary Threat(s): Unknown

Napa Western Flax
(Hesperolinon serpentinum)
Public Domain Photo from Creative Commons, Dr. Dean Wm. Taylor

Listed as Endangered by the California Native Plant Society (list B1.1)

Primary Habitat: **Endemic to California**, this annual herb is found in chaparral, and prefers serpentine soils.

Primary Threat(s): loss of habitat, agriculture, clearing, and grading

Narrow Anthered California Brodiaea
(Brodiaea californica var. leptandra)
Public Domain Photo from commons.wikimedia.org/

Listed as Endangered by the California Native Plant Society (list B1.2)

Primary Habitat: **Endemic to California**, this bulbiferous herb is found in broad-leafed upland forests, chaparral, cismontane woodlands, lower montane coniferous forests, and valley and foothill grasslands in the inner coastal range. It's found in Lake, Napa and Sonoma Counties.

Primary Threats: Residential development, foot traffic, and collecting, and competition with non-native plants.

Narrowleaf Milkweed *(Asclepias fascicularis)*
Public Domain Photo from Wikimedia.com

Primary Habitat: A common plant in California, it can grow in a variety of habitats and conditions. Milkweed grows in clumps beside roadways and on abandoned farmlands and other open areas. Along with being a host plant of Monarch butterflies, this forb also has a rich Native American cultural heritages, and was sometimes used to make cloth, and as a food source. The Yokia Indians of Mendocino County ate the young blossoms but not in large amounts. **NOTE:** the plants contains a mix of poisons that can induce vomiting and/or cause damage to the heart

Primary Threat(s): intentional removal by humans (it is harmful to livestock); often mistaken as "weeds".

Paintbrush, Indian Paintbrush
(Castilleja affinis)
Indian Paintbrush near Zim Zim Falls. Photo by Jim Rose.

Primary Habitat: This is a perennial herb that is **native** to western North America. And it's generally considered a "coastal" plant growing on hills and mountain slopes, but populations are also found inland throughout the state, including Napa, Sacramento, and Solano Counties. They bloom only briefly in June.

Primary Threat(s): loss of habitat due to development

Parry's Tarplant
(Centromadia parryi ssp. *parryi)*
Photo by Jake Ruygt and CalPhotos

Listed as Endangered by the California Native Plant Society (list B1.2)

Primary Habitat: **Endemic to California**, this annual herb is found in chaparral, coastal prairie, meadows, seeps, coastal marshes and swamps, and valley and foothill grasslands.

Primary Threat(s): Competition with non-native plants, agriculture, development, grazing, and road maintenance

Pipevine, California Pipevine *(Aristolochia californica)*
Photos by Mary K. Hanson

Primary Habitat: **Endemic to Northern and Central California** it's also known as Dutchman's Pipe, and grows primarily in riparian areas, along streams, ponds and rivers.

Pipevine can be found locally in Sacramento, Yolo, and Napa Counties. The American River Bend Park has an especially large population and is used as a natural "nursery" by California's Pipevine Swallowtail butterflies and their caterpillars. The plant contains a toxin that is present in the bodies of the caterpillars and butterflies, making them unpalatable to predators.

The vines appear first, then the flowers arrive. As the flowers die, the plant sprouts heart-shaped leaves and later generates multi-lobed seed pods. The seeds are nearly square and stack up inside the pods like bricks. When the pod dries, it breaks open and the seeds fall to the ground. The vines rise from rhizomes in the ground (and some can be over 20 feet long).

Primary Threat(s): intentional removal of the plants by humans; drought; herbicides.

Pink Creamsacs, Creamsacs
(Castilleja rubicundula ssp. *rubicundula)*
Pubic Domain Photo from Creative Commons, Barry Rice.

Listed as Endangered by the California Native Plant Society (list B1.2)

Primary Habitat: **Endemic to California**, this annual herb is found in chaparral, cismontane woodland, meadows, seeps, and valley and foothill grasslands throughout the northern inner coastal range. White and pink blossoms can be found on the same plant.

Primary Threat(s): Grazing, mining, vehicles, and road construction

Porcupine Sedge *(Carex hystericina)*
Public Domain Photo from http://commons.wikimedia.org/

Listed as Endangered by the California Native Plant Society (list 2.1)

Primary Habitat: This rhizomatous herb is found in marshes, swamps, and stream banks in the northern inner coastal range.

Primary Threat(s): loss or damage to watersheds, loss of habitat, drought, fire and expanding development .

Red Flowered Bird's-Foot Trefoil
(Acmispon rubriflorus)
Public Domain Photo from Creative Commons., Dr. Dean Wm. Taylor.

Listed as Endangered by the California Native Plant Society (list B1.1)

Primary Habitat: **Endemic to California**, this annual herb is found in cismontane woodlands and valley and foothill grasslands.

Primary Threat(s): Expanding development, grazing, and competition with non-native plants

Endangered in California

Red Mountain Catchfly
(Silene campanulata ssp. campanulata)
Public Domain Image from Wiki-Commons.

Primary Habitat: **Endemic to California**, this perennial herb is found in chaparral and lower montane coniferous forests, usually in serpentine and rocky soils.

Primary Threat(s): Loss of habitat due to expanding development

Rincon Ridge Ceanothus *(Ceanothus confusus)*
Public Domain Photo from Wiki-Commons.

Listed as Endangered by the California Native Plant Society (list B1.1)

Primary Habitat: **Endemic to California**, this evergreen shrub is found in closed-cone coniferous forests, chaparral, and cismontane woodland, and prefers volcanic or serpentine soils.

Primary Threat(s): loss of habitat due to expanding development.

Robust Monardella, Coyote Mint
(Monardella villosa ssp. villosa)
Public Domain Photo from Creative Commons, Jorg Fleige

Listed as Endangered by the California Native Plant Society (list B1.2)

Primary Habitat: **Endemic to California**, this rhizomatous herb is found in wetland areas, broad-leafed upland forest, chaparral, cismontane woodland, coastal scrub, oak woodlands, and valley and foothill grasslands. Locally is it found mostly in Colusa, Lake, Mendocino, and Napa County, but populations have also been noted in Yolo and Sutter County.

Primary Threat(s): Unknown

Round-Leaf Stork's Bill, Large-Leaved Filaree
(California macrophylla)
Photo by Andrew Borcher and CalPhotos.

Listed as Endangered by the California Native Plant Society (list B1.1)

Primary Habitat: This annual herb is found in cismontane woodland and valley and foothill grasslands throughout California.

Primary Threat(s): Urbanization, habitat alteration, vehicles, pipeline construction, feral pigs, and competition with non-native plants.

San Joaquin Spearscale *(Atriplex joaquiniana)*
Photo from Creative Commons, Barry Rice.

Listed as Endangered by the California Native Plant Society (list B1.2)

Primary Habitat: **Endemic to California**, this annual herb can be found among Chenopod scrub in meadows, seeps, playas, and valley and foothill grasslands, and prefers alkaline soils throughout western central California. Locally it can be found in Colusa, Glenn, Napa and Solano Counties. It blooms from April to October. Very little information is available on the ecology of San Joaquin Spearscale.

Primary Threats: Overgrazing and development, especially the conversion of alkali grassland to agriculture use.

Scalloped Moonwort *(Botrychium crenulatum)*
Public Domain Photo from Creative Commons, Eric White.

Listed as Endangered by the California Native Plant Society (list 2.2)

Primary Habitat: This rhizomatous herb is found throughout California and elsewhere in bogs and fens, freshwater marshes and swamps, meadows, seeps, and mountainous coniferous forests.

Primary Threats: Foot traffic, grazing, trampling, recreational activities, and road construction

Sambucus, Blue Elderberry *(Sambucus mexicana)*
Photos by Mary K. Hanson

Primary Habitat: This deciduous tree likes riparian habitats, stream banks, open places in the forest, oak forests, foothill woodlands, sub-alpine forests, coastal sage scrub and chaparral areas. It is found regularly in each of the five counties that comprise the Berryessa Snow Mountain region (Yolo, Napa, Lake, Mendocino and Solano County).

It is the host plant for the Valley Longhorn Elderberry Beetle.

The trees bear creamy white flowers in the spring and are frequented by a variety of pollinator species. It blooms from March through May.

In the summer, the trees bear clusters of dark blue/ purplish berries. The blue berries are high in Vitamin C and are edible, **but the unripe green berries and the red berries of other species are toxic.** The active alkaloids in elderberry plants are hydrocyanic acid and sambucine.

The elderberry is of well-known value to the Indians of North America and the many purposes it serves -- as a food source, dye and a source of folk medicine. The wood was often used to make combs and spindles, and the hollow stems were uses to make flutes and blowguns.

Primary Threat(s): Loss of habitat is the major factor.

According to the USDA: *"Western riparian ecosystems have been greatly altered by human activity. Riparian forests have been reduced to fragmented, discontinuous patches because of human intervention. For example, estimates are that 9up to) 90% of the natural riparian ecosystems in the U.S. have been lost to human activities. Regional losses in these ecosystems have been estimated to exceed 98% in the Sacramento Valley in California."*

When trying to reestablish elderberry populations the greatest threat has been competition with invasive plant and weed species.

Scarlet Larkspur (*Delphinium cardinal*)
Photo by Robert Potts, California Academy of Sciences

Primary Habitat: A perennial herb **native to California** and found only sparingly outside of the state borders, it grows mostly in the foothill woodlands and chaparral areas, and blooms between April and July. In the Berryessa Snow Mountain region, there are populations in Mendocino County.

Primary Threat(s): Unknown

Serpentine Cryptantha
(*Cryptantha clevelandii*)
Public Domain Photo from http://commons.wikimedia.org/

Listed as Endangered by the California Native Plant Society (list B1.1)

Primary Habitat: **Endemic to California**, this annual herb prefers chaparral and serpentine soils. It blooms from March through May and regionally is found most often in Colusa, Lake and Napa County. It's nickname is "glowing fly" because the new blooms are said tor resemble " blow flies ascending to the sun".

Primary Threat(s): Unknown

Shooting Star, "Mosquito Bill"
(*Dodecatheon hendersonii*)
Shooting Stars in Brophy Canyon. Photo by Jim Rose.

Primary Habitat: **California native.** Woods and prairies, from the valley floor to the yellow pine forests. A hardy perennial, it is not "frost tender". It is in flower from April to June, and the seeds ripen from June to July. The flowers are hermaphrodite (have both male and female organs), and come in a variety of colors from pink to deep rose and even red. The leaves a roots are poisonous if eaten raw.

Many populations have been found in the Cedar Roughs Wilderness along the trail, and in Brophy Canyon.

Primary Threat(s): Loss of habitat, Climate change

Showy Milkweed *(Asclepias speciosa)*
Photo by Mary K. Hanson

Primary Habitat: Showy milkweed is a **native** herbaceous perennial from widespread rhizomes, which produce stems that grow to 1½ to 5 feet tall in summer. It is hardy and can grow in a variety of habitats including in pastures, meadows, forest clearings, untilled fields, roadsides, and ditch banks. Milkweed stems die in winter, and new stems emerge in spring. The most common use for the plant among tribes of California was as cordage.

This plant is a common host plant for Monarch butterflies and their caterpillars.

Primary Threat(s): Removal by humans (the plants are toxic to livestock).

Slender Orcutt Grass *(Orcuttia tenuis)*
Public Domain Photo from http://commons.wikimedia.org/

Endangered in California, Federally Threatened

Primary Habitat: **Endemic to California**, this annual herb is found in vernal pools throughout northern California.

Primary Threat(s): Agriculture, residential development, grazing, vehicles, recreational activities, logging, fire, trampling, and competition with non-native plants

Small-Flowered Calycandenia
(Calycadenia micrantha)
Public Domain Photo from Creative Commons, Ken-ichi Ueda

Listed as Endangered by the California Native Plant Society (list B1.2)

Primary Habitat: **Endemic to California**, this annual herb is found in chaparral, volcanic meadows and seeps, valley and foothill grasslands, and occasionally along roadsides and in sparsely vegetated areas.

Several populations in Lake and Napa County, California.

Primary Threats: Road maintenance, fuel breaks, development, alteration of fire regimes, non-native plants, and feral pigs

Snow Mountain Buckwheat
(Eriogonum nervulosum)
Photo by Roxanne Bittman and the California Native Plant Society

Listed as Endangered by the California Native Plant Society (list B1.2)

Primary Habitat: **Endemic to California**, this rhizomatous herb is found in chaparral and prefers serpentine soils. It's found in Lake, Colusa and Napa Counties, and blooms from June through September.

Primary Threat(s): Energy development, mining, and vehicles

Snow Mountain Willowherb
(Epilobium nivium)
Public Domain Photo from CalPhotos, Ryan Elliot.

Listed as Endangered by the California Native Plant Society (list B1.2)

Primary Habitat: **Endemic to California**, this perennial herb is found in rocky soils in chaparral and upper montane coniferous forests. Found in Lake, Mendocino and Colusa County.

Primary Threat(s): Recreation, foot traffic, and logging

Sonoma Beardtongue, Mountain Pride
(Penstemon newberryi var. *sonomensis)*
Photo by Terry England and CalPhotos

Listed as Endangered by the California Native Plant Society (list B1.3)

Primary Habitat: **Endemic to California**, this perennial herb is found in chaparral and prefers rocky soils.

Primary Threat(s): Expanding development

Stoney Creek Spurge
(*Chamaesyce ocellata* ssp. *rattanii*)
Public Domain Photo from Creative Commons, Dr. Dean Wm. Taylor.

Listed as Endangered by the California Native Plant Society (list B1.2)

Primary Habitat: **Endemic to California**, this annual herb is found in chaparral and valley and foothill grasslands, and prefers sandy or rocky soils.

Primary Threat(s): Trampling, recreational activities, and vehicles

Tidytips, Common Tidytips (*Layia platyglossa*)
Photo by Mary K. Hanson

Primary Habitat: A California **native** growing only in the Western United States. It's found in many plant communities in the foothill woodlands, chaparral, grasslands, and yellow pine forests and blooms from February through May. The plants are often used for habitat restoration projects and attract many pollinators.

In the spring you can find large populations between Highways 16 and 20 in Yolo County. Tuleyome often hosts guided tours of this area in the spring of each year.

Primary Threat(s): Unknown.

Tule (*Schoenoplectus acutus*)
Photo by Mary K. Hanson

Primary Habitat: Tule (pronounced "too-lee") is a giant species of sedge that is common to wetlands and freshwater marshes all over North America. Native American tribes, including the Pomo and Lake Miwok tribes, used tule for construction and weaving purposes. Red-Winged and Tricolored Blackbirds like the tule as a basis for their nests and wrap nesting materials around the tule for added support.

Primary Threat(s): loss of habitat, water pollution

Twining Lily *(Dichelostemma volubile)*
Photo by Mary K. Hanson

Primary Habitat: A wildflower **endemic to California** it's also called a "snake lily" for the way it wraps itself around trees and shrubs. It grows primarily in mountain foothills, scrub and woodland areas. When in bloom, from April to July, each stem is packed with a head of up to 30 bright pink flowers. You can find them in Lake, Napa, Solano and Sacramento Counties.

The one in the photo was found along the Judge Davis Trail.

Primary Threat(s): Unknown.

Two-Carpellate Western Flax
(Hesperolinon adenophyllum)
Photo by Jake Ruygt and CalPhotos.

Listed as Endangered by the California Native Plant Society (list B1.2)

Primary Habitat: **Endemic to California**, this annual herb is found in chaparral and prefers serpentine soils in the inner coastal range. This plant can be seen in Lake and Napa County.

Primary Threat(s): Geothermal development, recreation, and grazing.

Western Larkspur *(Delphinium hesperium)*
Photo from westernwildflowers.com

Primary Habitat: This larkspur is **endemic to California** and likes grasslands, foothills, and woodland areas. Each plant can hold a few up to over 100 brilliant blue (or purple) flowers. Sometimes the flowers can also be pinkish or white. Native Americans and early settlers in California used the flowers to make blue ink. Locally, it can be found in Napa and Mendocino Counties.

Although beautiful, this larkspur is highly poisonous and ranks as "Major" on the California Poison Control scale.

Primary Threat(s): Unknown.

Wild Ground Iris *(Iris macrosiphon)*
Photo by Mary K. Hanson

Primary Habitat: This iris is **endemic to California** and grows in meadows, grasslands, foothill and oak woodlands, and mixed-evergreen and yellow pine forests areas. Large populations can be found throughout Lake, Mendocino and Napa County. The leaves are blue-green in color and the flowers can range from deep blue-purple to lavender and even yellow cream. The stems are usually very short and each plant produces one or two flowers. Blooming goes from March through May. The Pomo, Monache and Southern Yukuts of California used the seeds from this iris to make flour or meal (after leeching out the tannins).

Primary Threat(s): Removal of flowers from habitat by humans

Wild Onion, One-Leaf Onion
(Allium unifolium)
Photo by Mary K. Hanson

Primary Habitat: **Endemic to California** this perennial wild onion thrives in chaparral, grassy stream banks, closed-cone pine forests and mixed evergreen forests. It likes heavy soil and seems to do best in moist clay or serpentine soil. Regionally, there are populations in Mendocino and Napa County. Although the onions are edible -- The Pomo, Yuki, Wailaki, and Nomlaki used it as a food source -- you are cautioned not to remove bulbs from the wild as they are rather uncommon. The flowering heads display a ball of lavender-pink flowers between the months of May and June.

Primary Threat(s): removal of bulbs from the wild by humans

Woodland Clarkia, Elegant Clarkia
(Clarkia unguiculata)

Primary Habitat: **Endemic to California.** It thrives riparian areas, sun or shade in grasslands, woodlands, oak forests, and chaparral. Can range in color from white to pink to purple. Locally they can be found in Lake, Napa, Mendocino, Yolo and Sacramento Counties.

Clarkia is named after Captain William Clark of the Lewis and Clark Expedition

Primary Threat(s): Unknown

Black Oak, California Black Oak *(Quercus kelloggii)*

California Black Oak trees. Public Domain Photo through CalPhotos. Original photo by Charle Webber and the California Academy of Sciences.

Species is "Secure" at This Time

Primary Habitat: These **native** trees usually occur in mixed stands in north oak woodland areas, mixed evergreen forests and yellow pine forests, and can grow up to 80 feet tall and 4 ½ feet in diameter. (In "poor" sites, the trees can also very scrubby and close to the ground.) The crown is rounded and broad and the lower branches nearly touch the ground. Trunks are often forked, and the bark goes from smooth to thick, rigid and plate-like with age. Regionally, populations can be found throughout Lake, Mendocino and Napa Counties. The acorns are very large, and adult trees often act as a "nurse tree" to conifers. Leaves are "lobed".

Primary Threat(s): human removal of trees for development or firewood, overharvesting and deforestation, Sudden Oak Death, infestations by fungus or insects, over-collecting of acorns.

Public Domain Photo through CalPhotos. Original photo by Beatrice F. Howitt and the California Academy of Sciences.

Blue Oak, "Mountain Oak", "Iron Oak" *(Quercus douglasii)*

Blue Oak Trees. Photo by Mary K. Hanson.

Species is "Secure" at This Time

Primary Habitat: The blue oak is **endemic to California**, where it is found in open savanna and open woodlands with shrubby understories. At lower elevations it merges with annual grasslands, and at higher elevations it blends with chaparral, pinyon and juniper woodlands. It occurs in valleys and on low slopes of the Coast Ranges, on low foothills of the Sierra Nevada, and around the Central Valley. There are large populations in Mendocino, Sacramento and Napa Counties and somewhat smaller populations in Yolo and Lake Counties.

Leaves are small and slightly lobed. The trees usually have a single trunk (although forked trunks are also seen), and can grow up to 60 feet tall. The oldest know blue oak is 400 years old.

Primary Threat(s): Poor regeneration due to a variety of causes; livestock and wildlife herbivory, invasive grasses, drought, and probably other unknown factors.

Public Domain Photo through CalPhotos, by Jean Pawek.

Canyon Live Oak *(Quercus chrysolepis)*

Canyon Live Oak leaves. Public Domain Photo from Creative Commons, by Keir Morse.

Species is "Secure" at This Time

Primary Habitat: **Native** to California (but also found outside the state) this species of evergreen oak is found along creeks, canyons and slopes and in valley grasslands, chaparral, foothill woodlands, Lodgepole, Red Fir and Yellow Pine forests. Regionally, populations of the tree can be found throughout Lake, Mendocino and Napa Counties, with smaller populations in Yolo and Solano County.

The leaves easily identify it: they are oblong in shape with a pointed tip and round base, glossy green on top and yellow or gray (with age) on the underside. Native American tribes used the acorns as a food source (after leeching our the tannins), and the acorns are consumed by deer, squirrels, wood rats, harvest mice, and black-tailed deer... which makes the Canyon Live Oak forests prime hunting grounds for mountain lions.

Primary Threat(s): Unknown

Public domain photo from http://commons.wikimedia.org/

Gray Pine, "California Foothill Pine", "Ghost Pine" *(Pinus sabiniana)*

Public Domain Photos from Creative Commons. Original photos by Keir Morse.

Species is "Secure" at This Time

Primary Habitat: **native to California** these pine trees are suited to long hot summers. Found in chaparral and oak woodlands, they prefer rocky well-drained ground, but can also grow in serpentine soils. Regionally, they are found in Napa, Lake, Mendocino, Sacramento and Yolo Counties, and less often in Solano County.

The drooping needles of this tree are formed in bunches of three and can get up to almost a foot long. They're pale gray-green in color and are believed to be the only known food for a species of *Chionodes* moth. The trees generally grow about 45 feet tall, but can get over 100 feet tall in the right conditions. The pine cones are very large and heavy.

Regional conifer expert Michael Kauffman has some additional information on these trees at his website: http://www.conifercountry.com .

Primary Threat(s): Unknown

Knobcone Pine *(Pinus attenuata)*

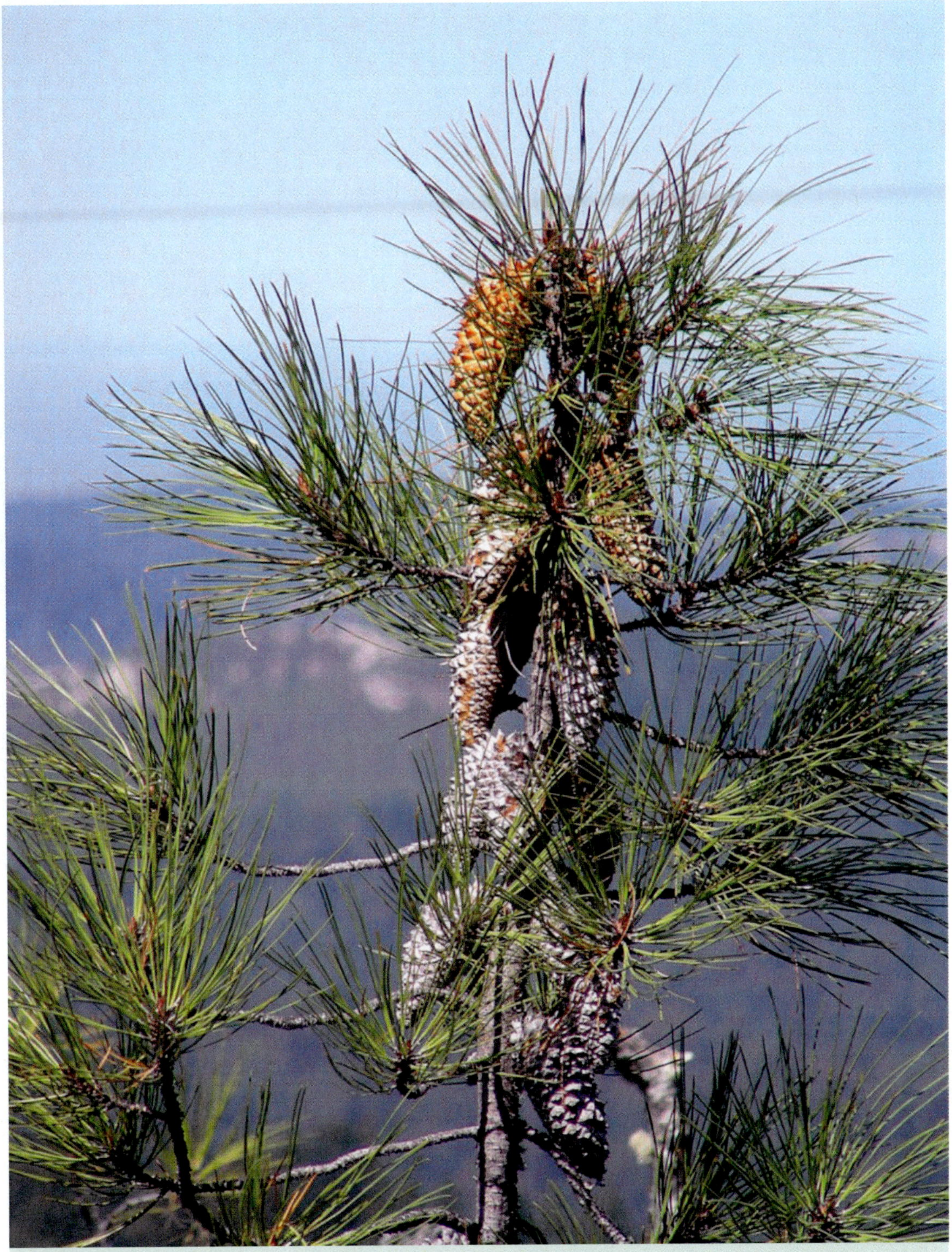

Public Domain Photo from Creative Commons. Original photo by Vicki & Chuck Rogers.

Species is "Secure" at This Time

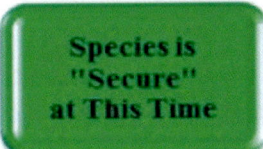

Primary Habitat: The largest concentration Knobcone Pines is in northern California, but the trees can also be found sparsely throughout the state. They're usually situated between areas of chaparral and woodland or higher elevation forests. The yellow-green needles grow in group of three and are twisted. The cones remain closed for many years which tends to leave them embedded in the trunk of the tree as it grows. The scales have a "stout prickle" on the end of them. Regionally, they can be found in Lake, Mendocino and Napa Counties.

Primary Threat(s): Unknown.

Konocti Manzanita *(Arctostaphylos Manzanita ssp. elegans)*

Photo Above by Jake Ruygt. Photo below taken at Boggs Mountain State Forest, Lake County by John Game.

Status – Listed as Endangered by the California Native Plant Society (list B1.3)

Primary Habitat: **Endemic to California** this perennial evergreen shrub is a subspecies of the common Manzanita. It prefers volcanic soils and can be found in chaparral, cismontane woodland, and lower montane coniferous forests. It's found locally in Colusa, Glenn, Lake and Napa County.

The nectar of its flowers is a food source for native bees and hummingbirds and it blooms between March and May. The flowers are later replaced by tiny apple-like berries. (The name "manzanita" means "little apple").

Primary Threat(s): Development of it habitat for urbanization, geothermal energy development, road widening, and suchlike impact on this manzanita. In some area they are also being lost when their range is converted into vineyards.

Manzanita, Common Manzanita *(Arctostaphylos manzanita)*

Most California species are listed as Imperiled by NatureServe

Primary Habitat: *Arctostaphylos manzanita* is **endemic to California**. It's found in chaparral, foothill woodlands and northern oak woodlands usually on slopes or in canyons.

There are actually 106 species of manzanitas, and 95 of them are found in California. All of them have smooth red bark and stiff twisting branches. *Arctostaphylos manzanita* leaves are shiny green, and its flowers are about ¼ inch long and shaped like tiny upside down bells or lanterns.

Flowers give way to small apple-like berries. The berries are edible in small quantities and are sometimes brewed into a tart cider.

The wood of the manzanita is very dense and hard. Although it is adaptable to toolmaking it not good for use as firewood as the wood burns exceedingly hot (and can damage some wood-burning stoves).

Common Manzanita. Public Domain Photo from http://commons.wikimedia.org/

Primary Threat(s): Expanding development, fire suppression, and shading and competition from invasive plant species.

MacNab's Cypress *(Cupressus macnabiana)*

McNab Cypress spray. Public Domain Photo from http://commons.wikimedia.org/

Species is "Secure" at This Time

Primary Habitat: **Endemic to northern California** this evergreen is usually found in the foothills and mountains, chaparral, and woodland areas. **The trees are found locally in Lake and Napa County, and the largest stand of them in the world is located on Walker Ridge within the Berryessa Snow Mountain region.** The MacNab Cypress is often associated with ultramafic soils.

It usually grows to a height of about 40 feet. The foliage is gray-green and forms in dense flat sprays that have a spicy-resinous scent. The seed cones are tight, like little fists, with small horns called "umbos" on them. The cones will not open until the tree is killed by wildfire.

Regional conifer expert Michael Kauffman has some additional information on these trees at his website:
www.conifercountry.com

Primary Threat(s): Expanding development

Public Domain Photo from http://commons.wikimedia.org/

Northern California Black Walnut *(Juglans hindsii)*

Leaves photo is a Public Domain Photo from Creative Commons, Vernon Smith.

Listed as Endangered by the California Native Plant Society (list B1.1)

Primary Habitat: **Endemic to California**, this deciduous tree is found in riparian forests and woodlands. Regionally, populations of these trees exist in Sacramento, Yolo and Napa County and smaller populations in Lake and Mendocino County.

Most of the specimens you see have been cultivated by native plant nurseries that use them as root stock and ornamental trees. **There is only one stand of confirmed native stock remaining,** and it is listed as Endangered by the California Native Plant Society. The trees grow to be up to 60 feet tall, with a single erect trunk. The nuts are covered with a tough drupe along with a thick brown shell that encases the nutmeat. Black walnuts are edible and have a slightly "earthy" taste.

Primary Threat(s): These tree hybridize easily and are being lost to hybridization with orchard trees; urban and agricultural development are also threats.

Photo by Mar K. Hanson.

Red Fir, Shasta Red Fir *(Abies magnifica)*

Public Domain Photo from Creative Commons. Original photo by Jean Pawek.

Primary Habitat: A **native** to California this is a "high elevation" tree usually found between 4500 and 9000 feet. The name "red fir" is derived from the color of the bark of the older trees. Of the red fir, there are two distinct varieties: including *var. magnifica* which is mostly in the Sierra Nevada. Regionally, there are a few stands in Colusa and Lake County. The trees are very tall, reaching upwards of 150 to 200 feet in height.

Primary Threat(s): Historically, these trees were greatly affected by logging and replaced by other faster growing conifer trees; development and other forms of land use were also an issue. Currently, the stands are either protected from logging in national forests/conservation areas, or are better managed by the logging industry to allow for regeneration of the species.

Sargent Cypress *(Cupressus sargentii)*

Sargent Cypress. Public Domain Photos from Creative Commons.

Species is "Secure" at This Time

Primary Habitat: **Endemic to California** this evergreen tree grows in forests with other trees, but also grows in chaparral and other mountain habitat. It prefers serpentine soils. Regionally, stands can be found in Lake, Mendocino and Napa County. *The largest Sargent Cypress stand in the world* **is found in the Cedar Roughs Wilderness area inside the Berryessa Snow Mountain National Monument.**

It normally grows about 35 feet tall but can get as tall as 50 feet or more when conditions are optimum. It takes the tree about 6 years to produce cones, and the cones require another 2 years to mature. Each cone contains about 100 seeds. Seeds are only released by wildfires or when the cones reach extreme old age and become desiccated. The trees themselves are somewhat fire resistant and can withstand one or two severe wildfires without substantial injury or death.

Primary Threat(s): grazing and trampling by livestock can kill seedlings; fire followed by overgrazing can eliminate cypress groves.

Scrub Oak, California Scrub Oak *(Quercus berberidifolia)*

Public Domain Photos from Creative Commons. Original photos by Keir Morse.

Species is "Secure" at This Time

Primary Habitat: This scrubby, short oak tree (usually between 4 and 10 feet tall) is **endemic to California** and is the most common shrubby oak in the Central Valley. It's an evergreen that grows in chaparral and oak woodlands throughout northern California and can tolerate a variety of different soils. These trees can be found throughout Lake, Mendocino, Napa, Solano and Yolo Counties.

Acorns are solitary or paired and start out green then ripen to a rich brown.

Primary Threat(s): Hybridization with other native and non-native oak trees; development.

Sonoma Canescent Manzanita *(Arctostaphylos canescens ssp. Sonomensis)*

Public Domain Photo through Creative Commons. Original photo by Dr. Dean Wm. Taylor.

Listed as Endangered by the California Native Plant Society (list B1.2)
Listed as "Imperiled" (S2) in the state of California

Primary Habitat: **Endemic to California** this perennial evergreen shrub prefers chaparral and lower montane coniferous forests in northern California's inner coast range. Regionally, the Sonoma Manzanita can be found in Colusa, Lake and Mendocino Counties.

This particular species, also called "Pink-Flowered Hoary Manzanita", is used a great deal in native gardening and landscaping because it doesn't take a lot of maintenance and looks lovely even in the heat of summer. Like all manzanitas it has mahogany-red bark, urn-shaped flowers and berries that look like tiny apples. This species' flowers are somewhat large and pale pink. All manzanitas attract pollinators, and some of them can even regulate their nectar to attract a variety of insects, hummingbirds, bees and other pollinators throughout the day.

Primary Threat(s): Native wild stands are affected by development and logging in areas where the trees are part of the understory.

Public Domain Photo from http://commons.wikimedia.org/

Sugar Pine *(Pinus lambertiana)*

"Big Bertha" is a Sugar Pine that dominates part of the landscape on Tuleyome's property on Goat Mountain. Tuleyome is also a land trust and purchases key properties in the region for conservation and educational purposes. Photos above by Jim Rose. Photo of the cone to the right is a Public Domain Photo from http://commons.wikimedia.org/

Species is "Secure" at This Time

Primary Habitat: **Native** to California, Sugar Pines can be found in mountain habitats and mixed conifer forests throughout California from the Cascade Range to the Sierra San Pedro Matir in Baja California. Smaller populations are found in the Coast Ranges of California. Regionally, populations are most dense in Mendocino County, but there are small populations noted in Glenn, Lake and Napa Counties.

They are the tallest and most colossal of the pine trees. They can live for up to 500 years (second only to the Giant Sequoia), and have the longest cones of any conifer. Their common name was derived from the tree's sweet resin which naturalist John Muir was quoted as saying was sweeter than any maple syrup he'd tasted. Commonly, these trees can grow up to 200 feet tall. Their needles are sharp, straight but slightly twisted and come in groups of five.

Regional conifer expert Michael Kauffman has some additional information on these trees at his website: www.conifercountry.com

Primary Threat(s): This species is particularly susceptible to "white pine blister rust" a disease caused by an invasive fungus, *Cronartium ribicola*.

Valley Oak *(Quercus lobata)*

Public Domain Photos from http://commons.wikimedia.org/, Phillip Bouchard.

Species is "Secure" at This Time

Primary Habitat: Valley Oaks are **endemic to California** and are often called the "monarchs" of the oak trees for their great size and beauty. They can live for up 600 years and are built to withstand wildfires. These oaks need a steady supply of groundwater to flourish, however, so they are most often found in oak/grassland woodlands and riparian habitat throughout the state. Their scientific name *"lobata"* is derived from their large deeply lobed leaves. They can be found throughout the region in Lake, Mendocino, Napa, Solano, Sacramento and Yolo Counties.

According to the U.S. Forest Service: *"...Remaining valley oak riparian and woodland areas comprise critical habitat which is intensively used by wildlife. Collectively, valley oak riparian forests support 67 nesting bird species, more than any other California habitat for which data are available. The state-threatened Swainson's hawk is closely associated with riparian habitat in the Central Valley, where these hawks use large valley oaks as nesting sites."*

Primary Threat(s): deforestation, development, conversion of forest habitats, water and forest mismanagement.

Western Redbud, California Redbud *(Cercis occidentalis)*

Western Redbud Tree. Photos by Mary K. Hanson.

Species is "Secure" at This Time

Primary Habitat: The Western Redbud is a **native**, drought tolerant tree that occupies a variety of habitat including oak woodlands, riparian areas, chaparral, and mixed conifer and closed-cone forests. The trees usually appear singly, but in riparian areas they sometimes form thickets. These trees can be found throughout the region in Lake, Mendocino, Napa, Sacramento, Solano and Yolo Counties and are also sold by native plant nurseries as ornamental plants for landscaping and gardens.

Between February and April, the trees bloom with sweet-pea-like pink or magenta blossoms. Their leaves are tender, heart shaped and bright green. **The leaves are a favorite of native leaf-cutter bees, and the flowers provide nectar for a variety of pollinators.** The Western Redbud reproduces by seed (and sometimes by bole after a wildfire), and the brown legume pods cluster in bunches, each one about 3 inches long.

Primary Threat(s): Unknown.

116

Common Fungi in the Region
include a variety of gilled mushrooms in all sizes and colors.
(All photos by Mary K. Hanson)

Best viewed during the rainy season, between October and March throughout the region.

All photos by Mary K. Hanson.

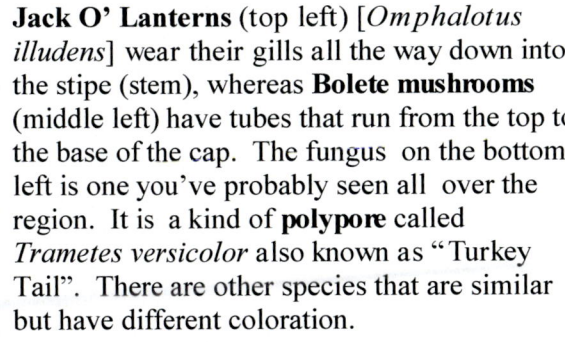

Jack O' Lanterns (top left) [*Omphalotus illudens*] wear their gills all the way down into the stipe (stem), whereas **Bolete mushrooms** (middle left) have tubes that run from the top to the base of the cap. The fungus on the bottom left is one you've probably seen all over the region. It is a kind of **polypore** called *Trametes versicolor* also known as "Turkey Tail". There are other species that are similar but have different coloration.

Elfin Saddles (Top Right) are the most common *Helvella* in the region and like to grow where the ground has been burnt. They can be black or white. **Cramp-Ball Fungus** (bottom right) on the other hand prefers to grow on dead and felled trees.

(All photos by Mary K. Hanson)

Cauliflower Fungus like this *Sparassis radicata* (top left) is more difficult to find and is supposed to be quite good to eat (once it's thoroughly cleaned) but it's also a parasite and grows off the roots of oak trees. It can grow up to "basketball" size and weigh around 50 pounds.

The next fungus (middle left) is related to Earthstars but is actually *Astraeus hygrometricus*, also known as the **False Earthstar** or the **Barometer Earthstar**. Like other earthstars it has a "puffball" center filled with spores. The leathery rays of the "star" are closed around the spore sac to start with, but when the humidity rises, the rays open and fold back, lifting the sack off the ground. When it gets hot, the rays can close up again to cover the spore sac. Spores are ejected through a vent on the top of the sac whenever the star is disturbed.

The third specimen (bottom left) is a kind of *Ramaria*, a **Coral Fungus** that likes growing in deep wet pockets between trees and in grassy gullies. Coral fungus in the region can be tan, brown, orange or red. These are supposedly edible, but may cause some gastric distress.

The yellow fungus seen below is *Dacrymyces palmatus* also known as "**Witch's Butter**" and it's a kind of jelly fungus. Jellies come in a variety of colors including yellow, white, black, brown and russet.

All photos by Mary K. Hanson

(Top left) Lace Lichen *(Ramalina menziesii)* also known as "Spanish Moss". On the right (from top to bottom) are Western Strap Lichen *(Ramalina leptocarpha Tuck)*, Hooded Tube Lichen *(Hypogymnia physodes)*, Elegant Sunburst Lichen *(Xanthoria elegans)*, and Gold Dust Lichen *(Chrysothrix candelaris)*. All Photos by Mary K. Hanson.

Often confused with fungi, these specimens are actually **lichen.** Lichen is formed by the symbiotic relationship between fungus cells and algae cells. Given the right circumstances, lichen can colonize almost anywhere on almost any surface, but you see them mostly associated with trees and stones. Fungi cells provide the hardy structure that can withstand long periods of drought, and the algae provides food by photosynthesis. In some forms of lichen, **cyanobacteria** (what used to be called blue-green algae) is also present and can pull nitrogen from the air that the other cells in the lichen can use as well. Because lichen are "compound" organisms reproduction processes can vary greatly from species to species. Some lichen reproduce by spore and others reproduce by "soredia" tiny projections that break off from the main body and then grow into new lichen masses.

Common Green Shield Lichen *(Flavoparmelia caperata)*.

Common Slime Molds of the Region

They are also often mistaken for some kind of fungi, but they're not; nor are they really plants or any kind of animals. They are slime molds. They start out as single celled organisms (rather like amoebas) that scour the ground looking for bacteria to eat. When conditions are right, they join together to form a communal "plasmodium", and then finally enter a "fruiting body" stage (like those in the photos) during which they produce spores (like fungus).

All photos are by Mary K. Hanson.

Wolf's Milk Slime Mold (*Lycogala epidendrum*)

White-Finger Slime Mold (*Arcyria cinerea*)

Chocolate Tube Slime Mold (*Stemonitis axifera*) turns brown as it ages, and is also called "Birthday Cake."

**TOP: Scrambled Egg Slime Mold (*Fuligo septica*).
BELOW: Insect Egg Slime Mold (*Leocarpus fragilis*)**

Habitat Systems within the Berryessa Snow Mountain Region

The California Department of Fish and Wildlife states that there are 59 distinct habitats in their California wildlife habitat database, but we will only touch on those that are specifically related to the counties within the Berryessa Snow Mountain region.

Aquatic Habitats: Watery habitats dominated by such plant-life as Water Moss, Algae, Duckweed, Eel Grass and Water Lilies, broken out into several sub-categories including Riverine (rivers and creeks) and Lacustrine (lakes). Animal life includes fish, turtles, frogs, mollusks, plankton, crayfish, crabs, tube worms, water-borne insects, nymphs and larvae, etc. Many other animals lay their eggs in the water (like frogs and newts). In this book, you can find aquatic species like the Clearlake Hitch, the Pacific Salmon, Rainbow Trout / Steelhead, and the Sacramento Perch.

Developed Habitats: These are habitats specifically developed for human use such as croplands, orchards, vineyards, and rice paddies; and also include urban and suburban areas and gardens. Depending on where the developed areas lie, they can be visited by animals from whatever other habitats are adjunct to the developed area, and they can supply food and shelter for a variety of different animals including birds, mammals, rodents, reptiles and amphibians, insects, etc. On the Conaway Ranch, for example, the rice fields are visited and inhabited by dragonflies and their larvae, waterfowl, Sandhill Cranes, sparrows, swallows, killdeer and other birds, beaver, deer and otters.

Herbacious-Dominated Habitats: These are habitats that include grasslands, wet meadows, vernal pools and wetlands areas. Plant-life includes Wild Oats, Soft Chess, Brome Species, California Oatgrass, Sedge Species, Tule, Rush Species, Tufted Hairgrass, Cattail, Bulrush, Redroot Nutgrass, and a variety of grass species. These areas that are too dry to support forests but have sufficient water to support herbaceous plants. There is generally one dry season and the area may be subject to drought.
- **Grasslands** are dominated by grasses but can also include sedges and rushes.
- **Vernal pools** are very temporary pools or ponds that provide habitat for distinctive plants and animals.
- **Wetland areas** are those that are saturated with water, either permanently or seasonally.

Non-Vegetated Habitats: These are barren areas where plants are virtually non-existent and are dominated by rocks, gravel and/or soil.

Serpentine Habitats: Habitats dominated by serpentine soils; soils that "weather from serpentine (serpentinite) rock that contains serpentine minerals (chrysolite, antigorite, lizardite, etc.). The minerals are composed of iron magnesium silicate. Serpentinite rock is a metamorphic member of the ultramafic family of rocks, derived from the earth's mantle, surfacing where oceanic and continental plates collide. Although serpentine soils occupy only one percent of California's land area, where they do occur, the serpentine syndrome... makes a striking impact on living landscapes..." [UC Davis Botanical Garden Newsletter, 18:12, 1993] Outcroppings are common in Lake, Napa, and Sonoma counties and can be readily seen along Cache Creek and Putah Creek. Since the soils are low in nutrients and high in chemicals not generally "friendly" to plants, the plants that manage to grow in these habitats are unique. The Sargent Cypress trees are one endemic species that can grow in these habitats.

Shrub-Dominated Habitats: These habitats include chaparral (mixed and montane), and shrub areas including alpine dwarf shrub areas. Plant-life includes Ceanothus Species, Manzanita Species, Bitter Cherry, Scrub Oak, Chamise, Coyotebush, California Buckwheat, and Sage species.
- **Chaparral** is often "on the side of the mountain" but can also include plans and foothills as well as mountain slopes. It is characterized by bushes and short trees (like mazanita). It is shaped by mild, wet winters and hot dry summers.

Tree-Dominated Habitats: These habitats include a wide range of different habitats from the subalpine regions up to the alpine regions such as coniferous forests, closed-cone forests, mixed forests, montane hardwood forests, oak woodlands, and riparian areas. Plant-life varies greatly depending on elevation and can include: Red Fir, Aspen, Mountain Hemlock, Douglas Fir, Sugar Pine, Pinyon Species, Juniper Species, Mountain Mahogany Species, Willows, Alders, Sargent Cypress, Canyon Live Oak, California Black Oak, Blue Oak, Interior Live Oak, California Buckeye, Black Cottonwood, Bigleaf Maple, White Alder, Cottonwood, Sycamore, and Valley Oak. Because tree-dominated habitats provide a lot of cover for a variety of different animal species, they are also some of the best hunting grounds for large predators such as raptors, bears, coyotes, mountain lions, etc.

Citizen Science: How You Can Help Scientists Track Species throughout the Berryessa Snow Mountain Region

Scientists love data, but they can't always be in the field collecting it. That's where you - the public - comes in. While you're out in the Berryessa Snow Mountain region, using this guide and taking photographs of what you encounter, you can also help scientists gather the much-needed data they require to track known species, discover new species, and see how climate change and other factors affect the regional environment. **You don't have to have any special skill or scientific degree to do this.** That's why it's called "citizen" science… it's information-gathering done by regular folks like you; folks who may be amateurs but who are out there in the environment making observations and recording information.

Just use your camera, pad, or cell phone to gather as many photos as you can while you're out exploring, and keep track of where and when you took the photos. Then load your photos and observations into any one of the on-line applications that can track the data. The most used and most user-friendly one is "iNaturalist", and it's FREE. You can even get an app for your cellphone for this one.

Just set up an account, and click on the RECORD! button. A screen will pop up that will allow you to upload your photos and their descriptions into the iNaturalist database. iNaturalist even provides help with identifying the plant or creature you've photographed if you're not sure what it is.

Once you have everything uploaded, it will look something like this ==>

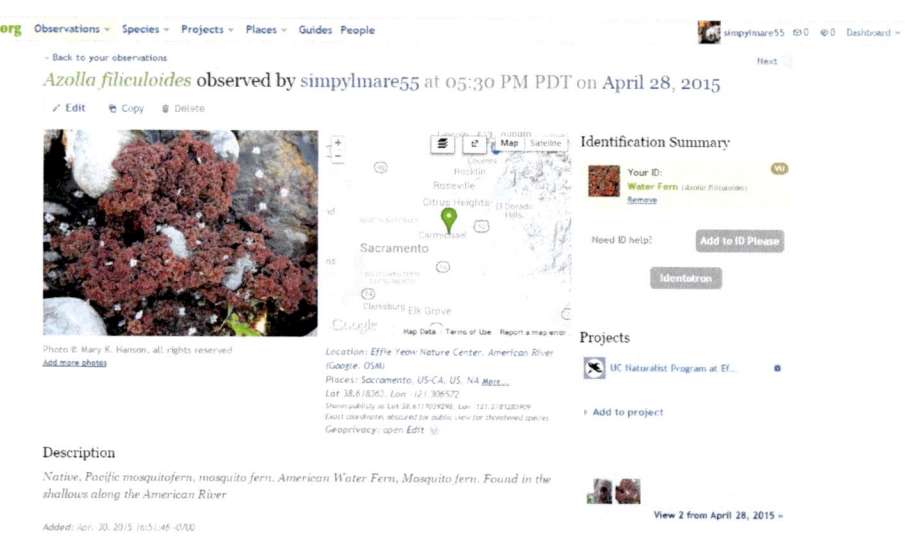

And there you go! You're now a "citizen scientist"!

Your participation in programs like this actually DOES provide a valuable service. According to an article published by the Cornell Lab of Ornithology, *"...In recent years over one hundred articles have been published, in peer-reviewed scientific literature that analyze and draw significant conclusions from volunteer-collected data. Many articles and book chapters describing learning outcomes for participants also have been published. Numerous publications document action outcomes as well, and offer strategies for linking research findings with management and decision making in different contexts…"*

This kind of activity also benefits YOU in that you learn to more accurately recognize and identify the plants, animals, insects and fungi around you… and you become more connected to the areas that you explore on a more personal and meaningful level.

DATE	TIME	LOCATION	DESCRIPTION
DATE	TIME	LOCATION	DESCRIPTION

Sources and Acknowledgments for the Species Guide

About Education.com. (2014). About Insects. Retrieved October 2014, from http://insects.about.com/

Audubon: The Climate Report, from http://climate.audubon.org/ and http://climate.audubon.org/sites/default/files/Audubon-Birds-Climate-Report-v1.2.pdf

Ancestry.com. (2014). Roots Web. Retrieved October 2014, from http://www.rootsweb.ancestry.com/~websites/

Birds.com, B. o. (2011). Beauty of Birds. Retrieved October 2014, from http://beautyofbirds.com/

Boxall, B. (2009, July 21). Blowing in the wind: Central Valley pesticides hurt Sierra frogs. Retrieved October 2014, from Los Angeles Times: http://latimesblogs.latimes.com/greenspace/2009/07/pesticides-hurt-sierra-nevada-frogs.html

Bureau of Land Management. (2014, October 6). In the Spotlight. Retrieved October 2014, from BLM California: http://www.blm.gov/ca/pdfs/cdd_pdfs/Dcco1.pdf

California Department of Fish and Wildlife. (2014). California Threatened and Endangered Plant Profiles. Retrieved October 2014, from https://www.wildlife.ca.gov/Conservation/Plants/Endangered/

California Herps.com. (2000-2014). California Herps. Retrieved October 2014, from A Guide to the Amphibians and Reptiles of California: http://www.californiaherps.com/

California Invasive Plant Council. (2006-2014). California Invasive Plant Inventory Database. Retrieved October 2014, from http://www.cal-ipc.org/paf/

Creative Commons Attribution 4.0 International. (2014). Creative Commons. Retrieved October 2014, from http://creativecommons.org/

Davis, K. a. (2010). Kim and Mike on the Road. Retrieved October 2014, from http://kimandmikeontheroad.com/

Eaton, E. R. (2014). Bug Eric.com. Retrieved October 2014, from http://bugeric.blogspot.com/

Fishbio. (2009-2014). FishBio. Retrieved October 2014, from http://fishbio.com/

Flicker Photos.com. (nd). Explore Recent Photos: The Commons. Retrieved October 2014, from https://www.flickr.com/commons

Hanson, M. K. (2014). The Chubby Woman's Walkabout Blog. Retrieved October 2014, from http://chubbywomanwalkabout.com/

Howard, B. C. (2012, September 28). National Geographic Society. Retrieved October 2014, from Clear Lake Hitch: Freshwater Species of the Week: http://newswatch.nationalgeographic.com/2012/09/28/clear-lake-hitch-freshwater-species-of-the-week/

Integrated Taxonomic Information System. (2014, September 29). Publication: U. S. Fish and Wildlife Service. 1993. Endangered and Threatened Wildlife and Plants; Review of Plant Taxa for Listing as Endangered or Threatened Species. . Retrieved October 2014, from ITIS Search Results: http://www.itis.gov/servlet/SingleRpt/RefRpt?search_type=publication&search_id=pub_id&search_id_value=7340

International Union for Conservation of Nature. (2014). IUCN Red List of Threatened Species. Retrieved October 2014, from http://www.iucnredlist.org/

Iowa State University, E. (2003-2014). Bug Guide.net. Retrieved October 2014, from http://bugguide.net/node/view/15740

Kauffman, Michael, http://www.conifercountry.com/ (2014) and http://backcountrypress.com/books.html

Mammalwatching.com. (2014). Mammal Watching.com Blog. Retrieved October 2014, from http://mammalwatching.wordpress.com/

National Audubon Society. (2014). Audubon: The Climate Report. Retrieved October 2014, from http://climate.audubon.org/

Nature Mapping Foundation. (nd). Naturemapping.org. Retrieved October 2014, from http://naturemappingfoundation.org/

Nevada Department of Conservation and Natural Resources. (2011). Nevada Natural Heritage Program. Retrieved October 2014, from http://heritage.nv.gov/taxon_detail/13952

New England Wild.org. (2011-2014). Go Botany: Simple ID Key. Retrieved October 2014, from https://gobotany.newenglandwild.org/species/potamogeton/zosteriformis/

New Hampshire Public Television. (2014). Nature Works - California. Retrieved October 2014, from http://www.nhptv.org/natureworks/california.htm

NW Blog Spot. (2013). NW Blog Spot.com. Retrieved October 2014, from http://nwbirdblog.blogspot.com/

Public Domain Images.com. (n.d.). Public Domain Images. Retrieved October 2014, from nd: http://www.public-domain-image.com/

Sherman, P. (nd). WP Clip Art. Retrieved October 2014, from http://www.wpclipart.com/

The Association for the Study of Animal Behavior. (2012). Western scrub-jay funerals: cacophonous aggregations in response to dead. Retrieved October 2014, from http://xcelab.net/rmpubs/Iglesias%20scrub%20jay%20funerals%202012.pdf

The Cornell Lab of Ornithology. (2011). All About Birds. Retrieved October 2014, from http://www.allaboutbirds.org/

United States Geological Survey. (2013, February 1). NPWRC Online Biological Resources. Retrieved October 2014, from Northern Prairie Wildlife Research Center : http://www.npwrc.usgs.gov/resource/

United States Geological Survey. (2013). USGS Multimedia Gallery. Retrieved October 2014, from http://gallery.usgs.gov/

University of California Davis, D. o. (2014). California Fish Website. Retrieved October 2014, from http://calfish.ucdavis.edu/

University of California, Berkeley. (2014, September 24). CalPhotos. Retrieved October 2014, from http://calphotos.berkeley.edu/

University of Michigan. (2014). Animal Diversity Web. Retrieved October 2014, from http://animaldiversity.ummz.umich.edu/

USDA NRCS National Plant Data . (nd). USDA Plant Guide. Retrieved October 2014, from http://plants.usda.gov/

US Fish and Wildlife Service. (2011, May 25). Federal Register. Retrieved October 2014, from Endangered and Threatened Wildlife : http://www.fws.gov/cno/es/pdf%20files/FiveYrReview2011.pdf

US Fish and Wildlife Service. (2013, July 2). Species Information. Retrieved October 2014, from Bay Delta Fish and Wildlife Office: http://www.fws.gov/sfbaydelta/species/es_kids_ca-red-legged-frog.htm

US Forest Service. (2013, March 28). Pacific Southwest Research Station. Retrieved October 2014, from Research Topics Wildlife & Fish: http://www.fs.fed.us/psw/topics/wildlife/herp/rana_boylii/

USDA Forest Service. (2014). Fire Effects Information System. Retrieved October 2014, from Species Search: http://www.fs.fed.us/database/feis/animals/bird/

Western Wildflower.com. (nd). Wildflower Trails of the San Francisco Bay Area. Retrieved October 2014, from Western Wildflower Plant Index: http://www.westernwildflower.com/plant%20index.htm

Wikimedia. (2014, 10 08). Wikimedia Commons. Retrieved October 2014, from Creative Commons Attribution/Share-Alike License: http://commons.wikimedia.org/wiki/Main_Page

Winer, A. (2010). Adam's Home Page. Retrieved October 2014, from Butterflies: http://www.adamwiner.com/

Xerces Society.org. (nd). Monarch Butterflies. Retrieved October 2014, from http://www.xerces.org/monarchs/

The Berryessa Snow Mountain region is part of the 4000 mile Pacific Flyway, the route taken by migrating birds from Alaska to Patagonia (at the southern end of South America). Between late October and February, the region is visited by a huge influx of migrating birds including Aleutian Geese, Snow Geese, White Fronted Geese, and Bufflehead and Northern Pintails ducks. The Pacific Flyway contains 60% of the habitat critical to wintering waterfowl in the region – and our area is ranked Number 2 on the list of the 25 most important and threatened waterfowl habitats in the entire continent.

In the photo to the left, hundreds of Pintail Ducks come in to winter in a local wetlands area. (Photo by Mary K. Hanson)

How You Can Help Restore Areas in the Berryessa Snow Mountain Region Damaged by the Wild Fires of 2015

The summer of 2015 was tough on many of the trails and large swathes of habitat in the Berryessa Snow Mountain region. The Wragg Fire and Rocky Fire decimated thousands of acres of wild land. Over the next several years, Tuleyome will be working hard to repair and restore damaged trails and habitats through our Home Place Adventures program. If you would like to join us and participate in trail restoration projects and/or habitat restoration projects in and around the Berryessa Snow Mountain National Monument, please go to our website at www.tuleyome.org and sign up as a volunteer.

The following is by Bob Schneider

Long-Term Planning
Tuleyome has participated in the FireScape Mendocino stakeholder planning process on the Mendocino National Forest (MNF). The goals of this planning process are to protect water quality and supply, restore forest health and fire to the landscape, mitigate for climate change, reintroduce jobs to the forest for local residents, enhance recreational opportunities and support the economies of local communities.

Some critical issues have been identified in this process that directly relate to fire safety. They are not new to forest health issues but we now need to specifically address them for our region.

These include:

- Fuel reduction and shaded fuel breaks: Where should these be located and how should they be accomplished?
- Fire Funding: There are both state and federal firefighting budgets. However, when these funds are depleted additional funds are raided from the National Forest operating budget. The irony is that funds that are slated for fuels reduction and building forest resiliency literally go up in smoke. We need a new protect the forest operating budget to accomplish what is needed for long term forest health and management
- Air Quality: As noted above we live in a Mediterranean climate with fire adapted landscapes. The region will burn and air quality is significantly impaired. Our choice as a society is to enable prescribed (controlled) burning; or wait for catastrophic wildfires. Controlled burning can occur at different times of the year and be less intensive. Currently, air quality regulations significantly limit prescribed burns. Fuels build up until catastrophic fires occur.
- Jobs in Forest: Forests must be sustainable over the long term. But, within that overriding principal there are opportunities to reintroduce jobs into the forest and support the economies of local towns. This can be work to restore forest health such as building shaded fuel breaks. This is might also incorporate organizations such as the California Conservation Corp or the Student Conversation Association,
- Community Safety: Communities and homeowners must ensure that they are fire safe. We must do our part before asking firefighters to risk their lives in wild fires.

Conclusion
One of the primary scientific reasons for the designation of the Berryessa Snow Mountain National Monument is to allow natural ecological processes including hydrology, fire ecology, conservation biology, wildlife connectivity, and climate change. The Wragg Fire and Rocky Fire provided a special opportunity to tell our story of fire science and fire-management practice and use this as a model for much of the West.

Associated Essays

- Scientific Conservation Values of the Berryessa Snow Mountain Region
- The Berryessa-Snow Mountain Region: Its Remarkable Geologic Features
- Protecting Water Quality and Supply And Restoring Resilient Forests in The Berryessa Snow Mountain National Monument

Scientific and Conservation Values of the Berryessa Snow Mountain Region

By Eldridge and Judy Moores, Susan Harrison, and Chad Roberts

The Berryessa Snow Mountain region of the inner northern Coast Range is part of a scientifically important region in California and North America. This region clearly demonstrates geological processes that were central to the formation of California's landscape: processes that continue to shape the land and the geography of the state today. In addition, the Berryessa region plays an important role in maintaining the conditions that make the California landscape one of the most conservationally significant environments in the United States.

Geologically, the Berryessa Snow Mountain (BSM) region incorporates deposits formed along the North American continental margin by interaction of three tectonic plates: the North American, Farallon, and Pacific plates. This region thus represents the geological history of more than 140 million years of plate activity, beginning with subduction (descent) of the Farallon plate beneath North America, followed by the mostly horizontal movement of the San Andreas transform fault system along the boundary between the North American and Pacific plates. During the years of subduction, a *"mélange"* of oceanic sediments, igneous, and metamorphic rocks, and exotic *terranes* from far-distant places accreted along the North American continental margin.

The BSM region includes the Coast Range Ophiolite, a remnant of ocean crust and mantle formed at an oceanic spreading center and emplaced on the western edge of North America. This ophiolite includes ocean crust made up of pillow basalts and bits of the upper mantle that typically include *"serpentine"* rocks, which are associated with some of California's resplendent biological diversity.

A dynamic story unfolds as one explores the BSM region. West of Winters, the sharply rising Blue Ridge and Vaca mountains contain nearly vertical layers of the *"Great Valley Sequence"*, sandstone and shale rocks that overlie the Coast Range ophiolite, containing debris shed from the North American continent to the east, deposited in ocean depths of about 3000 feet. Only a few places on the planet illustrate this scientific process as clearly as does the BSM region. Oil companies fly their geologists to California just to see and study the outcrop south of Monticello Dam. The layers exposed in the cliff along Highway 128 are similar to those found under hundreds to thousands of feet of water in the Gulf of Mexico and other deep-sea environments.

About 140 million years ago the ocean crust then west of the area that now holds Lake Berryessa (the Farallon plate) began to subduct under the North American continent. The subduction process in the Berryessa region continued for a very long time, adding an enormous amount of material (now called the Franciscan complex) to the western edge of the continent. About 30 million years ago, the spreading center between the Farallon and Pacific plates reached the subduction zone, and for the first time, the Pacific plate came into contact with North America. Subduction ceased along that intersection and horizontal motion (transform faulting of the San Andreas Fault system) began between the North American and Pacific plates, in the area that's now southern California. Over the eons, the transform fault has extended northward and continues today as far north as Cape Mendocino. The Wragg Canyon Fault, extending south from Lake Berryessa, is an active branch of the northern part of the San Andreas Fault system.

The former subduction zone, now known as the Coast Range Fault, passes through the Lake Berryessa valley, northward along the Eticuera Creek valley, and then continues northward to the western Klamath Mountains. The North American plate lies east of the fault, while west of the fault the Franciscan complex was formed by material scraped off the down-going Farallon plate.

Journeying around the west side of Lake Berryessa and northward along Eticuera Creek, one encounters outcrops of the shiny bluish-green rock known as serpentine and scattered areas of submarine volcanic rock ("pillow basalt"). These rocks represent part of the ancient ocean crust and mantle of the Coast Range ophiolite, now folded by tectonic movements related to the San Andreas Fault system.

The 140-million-year story told by the Great Valley Sequence, the Coast Range Ophiolite, the Franciscan complex, and the subsequent conversion of a subduction zone into a transform fault system provides a uniquely clear portrayal of the geological history not only of North America but also of many comparable plate boundaries around the world. This exemplary exhibition of world-class geology has been made available to the public, as well as to technical specialists, by existing access improvements in the Lake Berryessa region. These rocks are of *profound importance* for our historical and current cultural understanding of the geological processes that have led to the California landscape in this region.

The geological past affects the biological present in the BSM region. The variegated landscape, with its ever-changing elevation and differential exposures to sun, rain, and wind, and the range of geological substrates created by the accretion of a variety of rock types, have provided an opportunity for species occurring in California to develop significant diversity. This is particularly true for plants, including plant species that occur on serpentine substrates. This mineral is rich in iron and magnesium and poor in calcium, potassium, and phosphorus, and adaptation to serpentine substrates has led to the development of numerous species or subspecies of plants specifically adapted to these substrates.

The diversity of plant species in California, in part a result of the adaptations of plants to *serpentinitic* substrates, has led to the identification of the California Floristic Province as internationally important from a conservation perspective. While California's Mediterranean climate has played a dominant role in the evolution of this extraordinary diversity, regional topographic and substrate variations are a contributing factor. In the Berryessa region, the roles of Cedar Roughs and the serpentine outcrops in the Eticuera Creek basin are particularly noteworthy, but smaller serpentine outcrops are themselves often important conservationally. The widespread occurrence and overall distribution of serpentine exposures in the BSM region mean that the region is an important contributor to statewide biological diversity.

The diversity of habitat types in the BSM region supports a high diversity of wildlife species. Wildlife scientists universally recognize the significance for wildlife of riparian areas associated with aquatic areas (including streams, lakes, and ponds) and wetlands, including such sensitive species as Bald Eagle and red-legged frog. Studies suggest that as many of 75 percent of wildlife species in California are linked to aquatic areas and associated riparian zones. The BSM region also provides an abundance of oak woodland habitat areas, widely acknowledged by ecologists as among the most important habitat types in California, with more than 300 wildlife species directly associated with oak woodland habitat areas.

The greatest biological significance of the BSM region may arise from its location. The inner Coast Range, including the BSM region, forms part of the least-disturbed landscape framework north of the Sacramento-San Joaquin Delta for linking together natural conservation areas in California. The California Department of Fish and Wildlife and other agencies have identified the Berryessa Snow Mountain region as an essential habitat connectivity link in California, bridging together natural areas in the southern inner Coast Range and the eastern Bay Area with the extensive protected areas farther north and west in the Coast Range. Connectivity in the regional landscape is expected to be a significant factor in maintaining ecological resiliency in the Coast Range as climate change drives plant and animal species to adapt to altered temperature and moisture conditions. The conservation importance of the aquatic and riparian areas, the oak woodlands, and the habitat linkages in the Berryessa region cannot be overstated.

The geological and biological settings of the Berryessa region form parts of a scientific story to share with existing and future generations. The designation of the Berryessa Snow Mountain region as a National Monument gives permanent protection of the region and its important story. Our support for National Monument status for this special region and its story can and should be our legacy for future generations.

Dr. Eldridge Moores is Professor Emeritus of Geology at UC Davis, Judy Moores is Past President of the Cool Davis Foundation, Dr. Susan Harrison is Professor of Environmental Science and Policy at UC Davis, and Dr. Chad Roberts is a private conservation ecologist in Davis, California.

The Berryessa-Snow Mountain Region: Its Remarkable Geologic Features
Eldridge M. Moores and Judith E. Moores

The proposed Berryessa-Snow Mountain National Monument region (BSM) provides unparalleled access to geologic features associated with an ancient tectonic system where one plate descended beneath another. (See attached map of the Geology of the Berryessa-Snow Mountain Area.)

The Coast Range Fault, noted on the map, represents the ancient boundary between the upper North American plate and the descending lower plate. Rocks of the upper plate include Great Valley sedimentary and volcanic rocks overlying serpentine, that is, remnants of ancient oceanic crust). The upper plate represents part of the western edge of North America that formed 140-20 million years ago. Lower plate rocks include the Franciscan complex - deformed and metamorphosed (recrystallized) sedimentary and volcanic rocks - that were scraped off the down-going plate and buried up to 12-20 miles beneath the North American edge as the plate went down and then uplifted to the surface by erosion[1]. The active San Andreas Fault family was superimposed more recently on this earlier convergent plate situation.

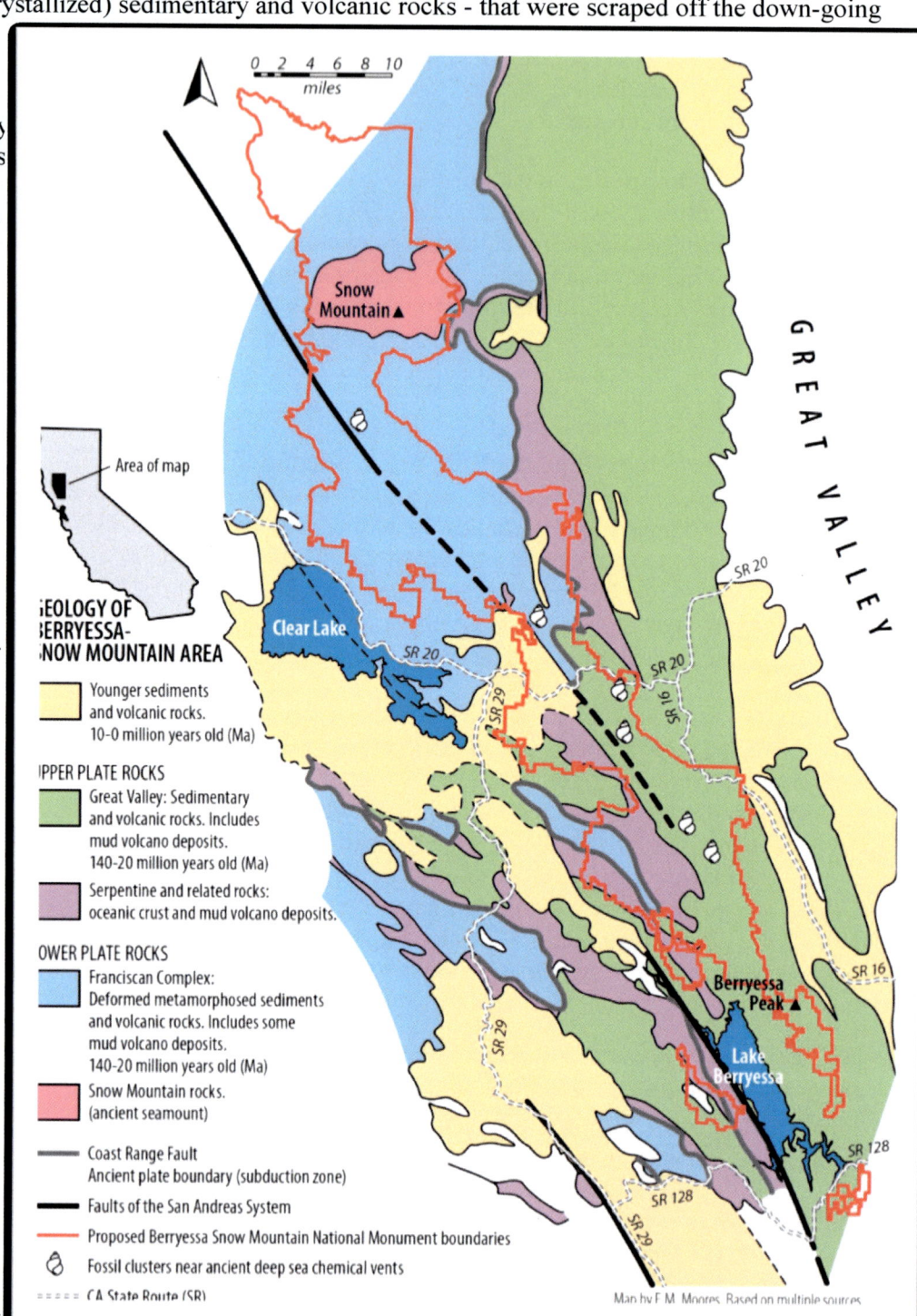

The Great Valley sedimentary rocks themselves were deposited originally on top of oceanic crust, which had previously been incorporated into North American continental rocks. Great Valley sediments were laid down in approximately 3000 to 5000 feet of marine waters at the edge of the North American continent. Subsequent earth movements tilted these rocks from their original horizontal position to steeply inclined vertical layers. These rocks are well exposed along the western side of the Great Valley, including in the southeast part of the BSM region.

The serpentine and related rocks of the down-going plate represent remnants of oceanic crust formed at an oceanic spreading center and subsequently added to the North American continent. Serpentine, scientifically called "serpentinite," is a rock formed by combining water with rock that originally was part of the Earth's mantle, the layer beneath the Earth's crust. Soils formed from serpentinite rocks lack certain elements required by most plants. Thus it is not surprising that the BSM hosts unique plant species in a variety of landscapes and microclimates that have adapted to serpentine-derived soils.

Some rocks of both the Franciscan and Great Valley units constitute blocky landscapes formed by a chaotic mixture of diverse rock types. Some of these rocks, often called "melange" after a French word meaning mixture, apparently formed as deposits of "mud volcanoes". Mud volcanoes are widespread in the Marianas trench area, where fluids derived from the down-going plate incorporate blocks of rock as they rise to the surface and spill over to form submarine earth flows some 20,000 feet or so deep on the ocean floor.[2] Some complex chaotic rocks found in the Great Valley and Franciscan units may have a similar origin. Other on-land exposures of similar ancient mud volcano deposits may be present in Turkey, Iran, Afghanistan, and SW Pakistan, but none of these areas is as well-documented or as accessible as the BSM area.

Similar tectonic processes are active today in various locations, *e.g.*, off the Pacific Northwest and in the Marianas Trench National Monument[3]. Such modern geologic rock-forming processes lie below thousands of feet of water and are not directly observable. To study such rocks, geologists employ deep-sea drilling, geophysical techniques of remote sensing, small deep-diving two to three-person submarines, or remotely operated submersible vehicles. In contrast, one can walk across the preserved fossil boundary between the two former plates in the BSM and see the rocks and geologic structures that formed during ancient plate interactions.

Snow Mountain itself represents a special feature. It contains submarine volcanic rocks, not more than 140 million-years old that look as if they were laid down only a few years ago. However, minerals identified in the rocks indicate that they formed as an oceanic submarine volcano (seamount) far west of California, then migrated with the down-going plate to the continental edge, were buried 12-20 miles deep, and rose again to the Earth's surface[4].

Also, the BSM area exhibits clusters of invertebrate fossils that apparently grew in deep water around chemical seeps[5]. Such clusters are widespread on some modern plate boundaries. The fauna live in the dark thousands of feet deep around cold to warm submarine springs that typically contain methane or hydrogen sulfide. The animals thrive, however, using the chemicals as nutrients. About six such ancient sites lie in the BSM area, enabling one to see such features closely and on land.

In summary, the geology of the BSM region provides valuable instructive exposures of features and processes of a convergent tectonic plate margin. Nowhere else in the world are such features as well developed, preserved, or accessible.

The proposed Berryessa-Snow Mountain National Monument region (BSM) is a unique region with world-class geology and biology. It is well worth National Monument designation.[6]

Notes and References
[1] e.g., Moores, E. M. and R. J. Twiss, 1995 (2014), Tectonics. Waveland Press, Long Grove, Ill., p. 144-150, 329-331.
[2] e.g., http://www.fws.gov/refuge/mariana_trench_marine_national_monument.
[3] Fryer, P., et al., 2000, Significance of serpentine mud volcanism in convergent margins, Geological Society of America Special Paper 349, p. 35-51.
[4] MacPherson, G. J., 1983, the Snow Mountain Volcanic Complex: an On-Land seamount in the Franciscan Terrain, California. Journal of Geology, v. 91, p. 73-92.
[5] Campbell, K.A., et al., 2002, Ancient hydrocarbon seeps from the Mesozoic convergent margin of California: carbonate geochemistry, fluids, and palaeoenvironments. Geofluids, v. 2, p. 63-94.
[6] Map drafted by Janice Fong of the UC Davis Department of Earth and Planetary Sciences.

Eldridge Moores is Distinguished Professor Emeritus of Geology at UC Davis. Judith E. Moores, an environmental activist, currently serves as a member of the Cool Davis Foundation Board. Email: emmoores@aol.com

Protecting Water Quality and Supply And Restoring Resilient Forests in The Berryessa-Snow Mountain National Monument

Chad Roberts, Ph.D., Pws, Esa Senior Ecologist
Conservation Ecologist

Summary

California is currently experiencing unprecedented drought and uncertain projections for future water availability under most climate scenarios. Consequently California must preserve the quality and maintain the availability of existing water supplies. Designating the Berryessa-Snow Mountain region as a national monument will protect water quality and a secure water supply by: (1) establishing regional coordination to protect critically important headwaters and tributaries to the Eel River, Stony Creek, Cache Creek, and Putah Creek, all of which provide important water supply to downstream users; (2) preventing new mining operations, which can significantly degrade water quality in a region already severely impacted by historic mining; and (3) bringing additional attention and resources to bear on the remediation of legacy mines that continue to contaminate local water supplies.

California, like most of the western United States, continues to experience both increasing wildfires and increasing costs of wildfire suppression. Fires not only result in human property damages, health effects, and loss of life, but also degrade water quality and diminish supply, damage natural habitats important for sensitive species, and increase the amount of carbon in the atmosphere. Consequently California must participate in the collaborative management of wildland fires on federal, state, and privately owned lands. National monument designation will result in a coordinated regional approach that will restore beneficial roles of fire in the landscape, prevent catastrophic wildfires, help to prevent water quality degradation because of wildland fires, and enhance the resilience of forests of the Berryessa-Snow Mountain landscape to the impacts of increased temperatures and drought resulting from climate change.

Background

California is in the midst of the most severe drought in state history (California Drought website 2015). In response, the State of California has undertaken the first-ever statewide restrictions on domestic water use as well as numerous other measures (Brown 2015).[1] The current drought has been linked to climate change, and climate change is expected to increase the risk of future water supply shortfalls in the state (Cayan et al. 2012; Diffenbaugh et al. 2015), particularly in watersheds in northwestern California and the Sierra Nevada (Thorne et al. 2015). Recent scientific assessments indicate an increased likelihood that climate change will lead to increasingly severe and long-lasting drought conditions in the American southwest (Cook et al. 2015). The intensity and duration of the current drought, combined with the increased probability of intense, long-lasting future droughts, means that local, state, and federal agencies must take actions to preserve the quality and reliability of the state's water supply, both for human uses as well as for the sustenance of the state's extraordinary environmental resources.

Climate change per se is an overriding consideration for landscape management on federal lands in the west. Recent projections (IPCC 2014) of future climate and related conditions (eg, sea level rise) incorporate benefits from potential mitigation approaches, but still indicate potential changes in temperature no less significant than those occurring in the Pleistocene/Holocene transition, although about 25 times faster. The clear importance of climate change for federal land management resulted in a Presidential Executive Order to incorporate climate change considerations into the management of all federal agency programs (Obama 2013). The significance of climate change for Forest Service lands in California, including Mendocino National Forest, is clearly indicated in the Region 5 Ecological Restoration Implementation Plan (USDA Forest Service R5 2013). At the present time the Bureau of Land Management has not presented specific plans for developing and implementing a similar ecologically focused restoration program.

---

1. It should be noted that the State of California has independently identified climate change as an extremely important cause of concern, and California is among the nation's leaders in developing and implementing approaches to mitigate its impacts. State programs are largely beyond the scope of this comment, but it should be noted that the state's adopted Fire Management Plan (BOF and CalFire 2010) is an important element in a joint fire-management program with federal agencies.

Climate change has been linked to changes in ecological conditions in wildlands throughout the western United States, including changes in fire regimes and intensities, increased vulnerability to attacks by pathogens and insect pests, and altered biological diversity at many scales (Sommers et al. 2011; Staudt et al. 2013). Increased temperatures alone result in higher moisture stress for plant species in forests and other ecosystems (Stephenson 1998), and the increased moisture stress has been identified as a source of mortality for trees of all species in forests throughout the west (van Mantgem et al. 2009) even without considering recent drought conditions. Projections of future climate in California have universally indicated an expected increase in fire, with both increased numbers of fires and area burned as well as increased fire intensity or severity (Lenihan et al. 2008; Westerling et al. 2011).

Virtually all aspects of federal land management are affected by climate change, leading to needs for new or altered approaches for a variety of contexts. For example, land management for sensitive species in both terrestrial and aquatic environments has historically focused on relatively static habitat designations. It's now clear that changing landscape conditions and ecological contexts requires a different approach. Recent summaries of the anticipated effects of climate change on California's native and alien fish (eg, Moyle et al. 2013) have identified a significantly increased risk of extinction for most natives, particularly species (such as those in northwestern California) that require cold water. Climate change also threatens sensitive terrestrial species with habitat loss. For example, the US Fish and Wildlife Service (USFWS 2011) has acknowledged a need for additional information and potentially different approaches to managing Northern Spotted Owl habitat in forestlands like those common in the Mendocino National Forest:

> "Given the complexity of the disturbance regimes in dry forest systems, response of spotted owls to these disturbances, and the projected influence that climate change will play on these regimes, this Revised Recovery Plan recognizes that active management of vegetation within the dry forest landscape is needed to restore ecosystem resiliency consistent with spotted owl conservation objectives. Restoration of forest ecosystems that are resilient to the endemic disturbance regimes and adaptive to impending climate change is a primary goal of any dry forest recovery strategy and needs to include some form of active management to achieve that objective. Our knowledge is far from complete, and management to restore these systems will be challenging. These knowledge gaps need to be addressed through a well-defined adaptive management approach that reduces biological risk to the spotted owl and provides information to inform future management decisions." (pp III-38/39)

Specific conditions that lead to the uncertainties identified in the comment above include a century of National Forest land management that excluded fire from its normal role in these forested landscapes. The primary result of this exclusion has been a vast increase in the abundance of small trees, which has had a net effect of vastly increasing two important forest stressors: (1) the accumulation of fuels within stands, which increases the risks of catastrophic, stand-replacing fires in those stands; and (2) a significant increase in moisture demand on all trees in the stand, which is the cause of the mortality in all species and sizes of trees described by van Mantgem et al. (2009) in forests throughout the west.

Increased temperatures, increased moisture stress, and increased fire risk will affect the ecosystems in all landscapes within the proposed national monument. Distributions of native plant species are anticipated to shift as a consequence of these changes (Lenihan et al. 2008; Hannah et al. 2012). At the present time the relationships with fire and drought that exist for shrubland/chaparral plant species within the northern inner Coast Range are not well understood, although it's generally acknowledged that these ecological systems differ from the better-studied chaparral areas in southern California; addressing this uncertainty is identified as a priority for Forest Service ecologists in the R5 Ecological Restoration Implementation Plan. While oak species that dominate California oak woodlands are well-adapted to living with fire (Plumb 1980), climate modeling has indicated that oak woodlands in the monument region may experience significant stresses from repeated fires and drought, resulting in distributional changes and/or conversions of oak woodlands to shrublands and/or grasslands. Climatic and water relationships that affect natural communities also affect other plants, and areas suitable for agricultural (eg, wine grapes) and private timberland uses are also expected to shift geographically during the coming century (Hannah et al. 2012).

Human community dynamics in the national monument region are also changing. California's population continues to increase, and the state's economy and culture continue to adapt to changing world economic and political conditions. The population in the national monument region continues to grow, which results in economic opportunities and stresses that affect the broader landscape. Recreational demands in the central California region that includes the Bay Area and the Sacramento metropolitan complex reflect both the increased population and the increased desire of many of these residents to participate in a variety of outdoor activities. At the same time, the desires of these citizens for an adequate energy supply and high environmental quality lead to conflicting pressures that affect the wildlands in the region, such as the conflict raised by air quality constraints that limit opportunities for biomass-fueled power production as well as limitations on the use of prescribed fires for landscape management.

All of the conditions and factors identified in this short summary are already affecting land management in the national monument region. Addressing the interplay among these factors as elements in the landscape that exists across agency boundaries is a critical element in developing a national monument management approach. This summary addresses the interplay among factors affecting water quality and supply and the opportunities for restoring forest health presented by fire management in the region, in a time when climate change is rewriting the relationships of processes operating on the landscape.

PRESERVING WATER QUALITY AND SUPPLY
The Berryessa-Snow Mountain region contains headwaters of streams that flow into Stony Creek, Cache Creek, Putah Creek, and the Eel River. These waterbodies are a significant water source for agriculture and domestic water users in northern California adjacent to the proposed monument, and they form part of the primary catchment for water users farther downstream. Stony Creek, Cache Creek, and Putah Creek all provide water for the western Sacramento River basin and the Sacramento-San Joaquin Delta, and thus for water users in the southern Central Valley and southern California. The Eel River headwaters diverted through the Potter Valley Project supply much of the summer flow in the Russian River basin for Mendocino and Sonoma counties; these streams also provide flows that sustain ecological processes in the Eel River basin below Cape Horn Dam. Protection of the headwaters within the monument will have important benefits on the quality and supply of water for many people in California.

Water supply concerns have been identified for California that stem from the uncertain effects of climate change and drought. It remains unclear how hydrological patterns in California will be affected by climate change, although there's near consensus that snowfall will decrease. Recent hydrological modeling (Thorne et al. 2015; Diffenbaugh et al. 2015) has indicated that substantial decreases in rainfall should be expected by the end of the century from most of the mountainous watersheds in California, including those in the national monument area.

Assuring adequate water for California's population requires a balanced consideration of quality as well as quantity. Actions or conditions that degrade water quality reduce the amount of water available for human use, or increase its cost because of requirements for additional treatment. Wildland fire typically exerts a significant detrimental effect on water quality (Bladon et al. 2014), and therefore a primary concern in the monument region is to reduce the extent and/or severity of wildland fire (see following section for additional considerations). Additional adverse effects on water quality sometimes occur as a result of land use management, particularly from roads, or from improperly managed actions such as grazing, mining, or timber harvesting.

The Berryessa-Snow Mountain landscape also provides water to sustain important natural aquatic areas and fishery resources. East- and south-draining stream basins are tributary to the Sacramento River system and the Delta, and have fewer native fish species and more alien species than do the west-draining basins, which are branches of or tributaries to the Eel River. Habitat conditions in these river systems differ substantially, with many of the Sacramento tributaries having lower and warmer summertime flows than do Eel River elements. Accordingly the two systems exhibit substantially different fishery profiles. Descriptions of the fish communities in these systems are beyond the scope of this comment, but in general the Sacramento system includes many species that tolerate or even thrive in warm water, whereas most species in the Eel system require relatively cold water. In a functional sense these fish communities have evolved to "fit" the conditions that the river systems provide.

The aquatic condition in each tributary stream (in both systems) is dependent on the volume, flow rate, and other characteristics of the stream. Absent sufficient flow, instream habitat conditions may become "degraded" for species that require cold water. Water temperature, dissolved oxygen, and various discharge-related physical parameters of the streambeds are significant determinants of habitat conditions (Thompson and Larsen 2004), and therefore of the fish species that can subsist in each stream. The ability of the basin to provide these necessary habitat conditions (water quality and quantity) is no less a function of the health of the watersheds than is the usefulness of the streams for human purposes.

Riparian areas associated with the streams and other aquatic features are essential elements of aquatic systems. Characteristically riparian areas include stream floodplains and other areas that provide allochthonous material to stream channels (Naiman et al 2000; many references). Ecologically the riparian areas form part of an interconnected system that includes water flowing in the stream, below the stream channel (hyporheic flow), and in the floodplain, all of which are hydrologically linked (National Research Council 2002). In other words the quality of riparian areas is fundamentally linked to the quality of the stream, and riparian areas actually constitute elements in the aquatic systems that exchange water with and provide organic material and physical substrate elements to the stream channels. While riparian areas may be shrubby or even grass-dominated, they are frequently composed of tall woody vegetation that may shade a stream channel and help to moderate water temperature. Riparian areas capture sediment and other pollutant materials before they reach the aquatic areas, and riparian vegetation often provides key structural elements that strengthen and stabilize floodplain margins against the effects of high flows. For all of these reasons riparian areas are as dependent on the quality and quantity of water reaching the riparian area as are the instream resources.

While the lands within the Berryessa-Snow Mountain region have been subjected to many intensive land uses during past centuries, the region still contains significant unroaded lands within and around the Snow Mountain Wilderness Area. Roadless areas have important environmental values and are recognized as sources of clean water (USDA Forest Service 2001). Roads can significantly affect water quality and stream flows (Gucinski et al. 2001). Anderson et al. (2012) assessed the relationship of watershed condition and land management status and found a strong spatial association between watershed health and protective designations. DellaSala et al. (2011) found that unroaded forest lands provide "a valuable and increasingly rare natural supply of abundant, clean, and naturally reliable water… affordable drinking water for municipal and rural communities; water for agricultural and industrial uses…aquifer recharge; flood protection; reliable water supply…and, increasingly, the vitality and sustainability of local economies."

Balancing land uses in the national monument is an overriding concern for the management plan that will be developed following designation. Intrinsic trade-offs exist involving such uses as vegetation management and prescribed fire that will be required in order to manage forest health, while at the same time there's a strong desire to protect other resources like abundant water supplies. For example, recent considerations have reawakened the notion that reducing tree cover in forests may be an approach that could increase water yield, although it has been projected that climate warming will result in increased transpiration by abundant vegetation that may substantially reduce water yields from forests (Goulden and Bales 2014). The national monument proposal assumes the existence of such potentially conflicting needs in specifying the inclusion of multiple stakeholders in the advisory group for the development of the management plan.

Other significant water quality concerns exist within the national monument region. During the California gold rush the highest density of mercury mines in the state occurred within the region. Many of the waterbodies in the monument region are contaminated by mercury generated from mining waste (see Central Valley RWQCB [2005] for a synopsis of mercury's impacts on water quality and health and a discussion of regulatory options pursuant to the Clean Water Act [CWA] and the state's Porter-Cologne Act). In 2011, the California Department of Toxic Substances Control (CDTSC) reviewed existing research on 82 mine sites and found that many were significant sources of mercury contamination in local water supplies (CDSTC 2011). Key findings of studies reviewed by CDSTC include:
- Past and ongoing mercury releases from mines have contaminated soil and water throughout the Cache Creek Watershed, with contaminants reaching as far as the Sacramento-San Joaquin Delta and San Francisco Bay.
- Several waterbodies within the Cache Creek watershed are "impaired" pursuant to CWA section 303 due to mercury contamination.
- Bioaccumulation of mercury threatens human and animal health in Cache creek, the Sacramento River, Sacramento-San Joaquin Delta, and San Francisco Bay.
- The Sulphur Bank Mercury Mine, within the Cache Creek Watershed, has been placed on the National Priorities List for pollution remediation.

The CDTSC report highlights the importance of controlling ongoing releases from mine sites as being "essential prior to attempting to clean up the creek system below the release points." Preventing new sources of pollution is also essential to facilitate waterbody clean-up.

The national monument proposal was crafted with full awareness of the relationships and issues summarized in this section. Regional water quality and water supply concerns are embedded in many agency and public processes in California (California DWR 2015). By engaging stakeholders in the regional planning process the monument's implementation will identify short-term and long-term concerns for water quality and supply, and appropriate solutions can be enacted locally, or regionally throughout the monument, as needed. Implementation will include developing practices that prevent water quality degradation that could occur because of grazing, mining, logging, road construction, and similar land uses, which must be subordinate to the conservation purposes identified in section 3(b) of the proposal. By preventing new mining claims, monument designation will prevent new sources of mining contamination within the waterbodies of the Berryessa-Snow Mountain region. Monument designation can also lead to the reclamation of abandoned mines, reducing contamination and improving water quality in streams and reservoirs listed for mercury pollution under the Clean Water Act, including water supply reservoirs in Lake Berryessa, Clear Lake, and Indian Valley Reservoir.

FIRE, CLIMATE RESILIENCE, AND REGIONAL CONSERVATION IN THE BERRYESSA-SNOW MOUNTAIN LANDSCAPE

It's no longer possible to consider conservation planning without including climate change (Staudt et al. 2013, National Wildlife Federation 2015), and in the western US it's not possible to consider climate change or conservation planning without including fire management (McKenzie et al. 2004; many subsequent references). The national monument proposal has incorporated regional conservation planning issues since its inception, and they are already a focus of extensive stakeholder involvement through the FireScape program and other outreach. Conservation planning and landscape resilience in the national monument region incorporate recognition of the extraordinary range of ecological variability in the region, overlaying climate-driven changes in temperature and moisture, and the potential effects of increased fire, as factors that are already altering regional ecological processes and which will become more significant as this century unfolds.

The monument incorporates a significant natural ecological transition zone, located approximately north of Clear Lake and extending northeast along the Central Valley (USEPA Western Ecology Division 2015). In general, the forested landscape in the Mendocino National Forest is part of an ecoregion (Klamath Mountains and California High North Coast Range) different from the lower Inner Coast Range ecoregion to the south (Central California Foothills and Coastal Mountains). The ecoregion difference is related to dominance in the Klamath bioregion and high Coast Ranges by ecological communities that are composed mostly of coniferous forests, while the biotic communities in the lower Coast Ranges are mostly dominated by chaparral and oak woodlands. This distinction results in substantial differences in local management concerns, full consideration of which is beyond the scope of this comment. However, the general focus of conservation management in the region tracks the "BACKGROUND" summary above.

Fire and conservation concerns are most fully developed in the forested landscape north of Clear Lake. These forests, like other National Forests in the west, have experienced increased fires in recent decades, generally a consequence of long-established USDA Forest Service fire-management policy. The "natural" fire regime in this forested landscape included relatively common low-intensity fires that likely removed many of the smaller and younger trees and most shrubs from the forests (Skinner et al 2009), a finding typical of most western forestlands and one that

Stand structures in "dry" (A) and "mesic" (B) forest stands, Mendocino National Forest (from Skinner et al 2009). Note the densities of small-diameter stems, likely a consequence of fire suppression policies. See text for discussion.

has been amplified by other fire-ecology studies in the Klamath bioregion (Taylor and Skinner 2003; Halofsky et al. 2011). Forest stands in the Mendocino National Forest today typically include abundant small trees (see figure), regardless of their status as "mesic" or "dry" (Skinner et al. 2009). The abundance of small trees in these stands increases moisture stress on all trees in these stands, leading to increased mortality of trees in all size classes; increases the ladder fuels in these stands, increasing the likelihood that a low-intensity ground fire will reach the canopy and become a high-intensity fire; and allows stands to become dominated by "shade-tolerant" species that fare less well following a fire and increasing the likelihood that a fire will lead to a non-forested condition in the warmer, dryer future.

Adaptive management approaches in western forests incorporate a number of approaches to reduce fuel loadings and increase resilience in stands such as those shown in the figure, including thinning, controlled fire, and mastication. A number of factors enter into the selection and implementation of appropriate fuels management approaches, including management purposes, initial and desired future stand structure, tree species composition, and cost. Managers have found that it's possible to produce desired management goals (eg, retention of large trees as elements of habitat for late-seral wildlife) through the selection and implementation of a variety of forest management practices (a result long-predicted by Jerry Franklin's "ecological forestry" approaches; see Franklin et al. 2007). The application of a variety of fuels management treatments in the Northern Sierra Nevada has increased forest resilience while also meeting management objectives for wildlife habitat (including sensitive species), water quality, and biomass production (Stephens et al. 2014). Similar approaches are currently elements of discussion for the national monument region as part of the FireScape Mendocino program. This effort should be recognized as an implementation of the Forest Service Region 5 Ecological Restoration Implementation Plan, in addition to being an early implementation of the goals for the monument.

Restoration of the ecological health to forests in the monument, or elsewhere in the west, is not a short-term effort, and requires (as described in the Northern Spotted Owl Recovery Plan [USFWS 2011]) "active management of vegetation," in which anticipated future conditions help guide the selection of management approaches. Given the effects of climate change and drought already impacting western landscapes, the implementation of informed fuels-management approaches and management to increase resilience to fire in forests of the monument region simply cannot await an auspicious future moment; there is an urgency that mandates immediate action. The increased emphasis on conservation and increased funding resulting from monument designation will aid in the regional development and implementation of adaptive management and conservation-based approaches.

The monument region also includes non-forested areas that have substantial conservation value and for which active management to preserve those values is required. Much of the monument region is dominated by shrublands ("chaparral"), an ecosystem type not well understood ecologically in the northern interior Coast Range, but which appears to function differently from the chaparral and coastal scrub ecosystems in southern California (Keeley 2002). As noted above, the Forest Service identified in it Ecological Restoration Implementation Plan a need for increased research attention on shrublands in northern California. Monument designation will assist in sharpening that focus and extending it to BIM lands. This is a particularly desirable conservation outcome for the monument region owing to the importance in the region of serpentinitic substrates and the flora that are adapted to them (see Harrison and Rajakaruna 2011 for examples and details).

As noted previously, the impacts of climate change on oak habitats in the monument region are not well understood. Several climate modeling studies have indicated a high probability that most lowland areas within the monument region will not be climatically suitable oak woodlands by the end of the century (eg, Hannah et al. 2012 and other studies cited therein). Currently the federal lands in the monument don't include large areas of oak woodlands, but projections of future conditions (eg, Lenihan et al. 2008) indicate that much of the monument area suitable for oak woodlands by the end of the century will occur on federally owned land. An important element in planning the ecological landscape of 2100 is what role the federal agencies should play in the development of these future conditions (eg, see Lawler and Olden 2011).

A primary element underlying the national monument proposal has always been the ecological transitions that must occur in the region in order to accommodate future climate-forced ecological patterns. A primary element in those plans must be the development and enhancement of ecological connectivity throughout the monument region, a factor that has been identified by many conservation scientists (eg, Spencer et al 2010) and agencies (eg, CDFW website 2015). It's no longer clear that conservation strategies that rely on fixed habitat networks will enable adjustments to climate-altered habitats. At the present time there is no coherent strategy in place in the region that addresses these transitions, a shortcoming that clearly can only be addressed through monument designation and the subsequent development of multi-agency management plans.

Resilient landscapes also are important for meeting other objectives. For example, healthy forests play an important role in maintaining water quality and ensuring stream flows late into the season (Troendle and Olsen 1994). Some forests in the Berryessa-Snow Mountain region have been degraded by past management activities and fire suppression (USDA 1995). As noted above, fires in forestlands can have significant adverse effects on water quality (Bladon et al. 2014, Paige and Zygmunt 2013, USDA 2011). Restoring the forests of the Berryessa-Snow Mountain national monument to a healthy condition will help maintain water quality and supply.

The Mendocino National Forest is currently engaged in an "all lands" planning process, called FireScape Mendocino, which addresses forest health through a restoration of more natural fire regimes and forest stand structure (at the present time the BLM is not a core member of the FireScape Mendocino program, although it should be noted that the California Department of Forestry and Fire Protection [CalFire] is a member). This program is an element of the Fire Learning Network (FLN)[2]. The FireScape Mendocino project is already engaged in multi-agency and multi-stakeholder discussions about the issues summarized above.

The FireScape project area includes essentially all of Mendocino National Forest, as well as BLM lands north of Highway 20 and elsewhere near the Forest's boundaries on both eastern and western sides of the Forest, Native American lands, and private lands that adjoin the National Forest in parts of six California counties. The collaborative process embodied in FireScape Mendocino exemplifies the multi-stakeholder approach adopted for planning the national monument proposal, and it represents an early implementation of the process that will be involved in developing the management plan for the monument. A national monument designation will provide additional resources (including funding) to assist in implementing this "all-hands" engagement of agencies and other stakeholders.

BENEFITS FROM NATIONAL MONUMENT DESIGNATIONS IN CALIFORNIA
California is blessed with several national monuments, each of which has been established to preserve natural or cultural resources. Management of these monuments provides good analogs for discerning benefits of national monument designation on concerns considered in this comment.

President Clinton established the Giant Sequoia National Monument in April 2000 (Clinton 2000). The purpose of the monument was to protect the giant sequoia forest ecosystems, as well as the diverse array of plant and animal habitats that accompany those ecosystems. Additionally, the proclamation highlighting the monument highlighted the need to restore forest ecosystems:
> "These giant sequoia groves and the surrounding forest provide an excellent opportunity to understand the consequences of different approaches to forest restoration. These forests need restoration to counteract the effects of a century of fire suppression and logging. Fire suppression has caused forests to become denser in many areas, with increased dominance of shade-tolerant species.
> Woody debris has accumulated, causing an unprecedented buildup of surface fuels. One of the most immediate consequences of these changes is an increased hazard of wildfires of a severity that was rarely encountered in pre-EuroAmerican times. Outstanding opportunities exist for studying the consequences of different approaches to mitigating these conditions and restoring natural forest resilience."

The current management plan for the monument highlights the emphasis on forest restoration and proposes a suite of fuel reduction and restoration activities within the monument. "The proposed fuel reduction activities in the selected

---

2. Participating entities are identified on the Nature Conservancy's FLN Conservation Gateway website (https://www.conservationgateway.org/ConservationPractices/FireLandscapes/FireLearningNetwork/Pages/fire-learning-network.aspx; accessed 15 May 2015): "The Fire Learning Network, launched in 2002, is a joint project of **The Nature Conservancy**, the **USDA Forest Service** and several agencies of the **US Department of the Interior** (Bureau of Indian Affairs, Bureau of Land Management, Fish & Wildlife Service and National Park Service)."

alternative are expected to reduce surface and ladder fuels, modifying fire behavior and resulting in fuel conditions that move toward the desired condition" (USDA 2012). The plan further states:

"The selected alternative will decrease fuel buildups and reduce the risk of uncharacteristically severe wildfires, which may threaten the objects of interest. It will be effective over the long term in restoring the desired fire characteristics of generally low susceptibility to stand-replacing fires and a more frequent and low-intensity fire return interval in fire-dependent ecosystems. This will lead to greater species diversity, a mosaic of tree sizes and ages, and therefore to landscapes that are more resilient and adaptable to environmental change."

The Forest Service identified a desired future condition within the forests of the monument:

"Fire occurs in its characteristic pattern and resumes its ecological role…Fire susceptibility and severity, and fire hazards to adjacent human communities and surrounding forest types, are low. The need to maintain fuel conditions that support fires characteristic of complex ecosystems is emphasized and allows for a natural range of fire effects in the Monument."

Other national monuments in California also emphasize restoring degraded ecosystems. Within the Carrizo Plain National Monument, for example, the BLM aims to maintain the role of fire in the ecosystem where feasible, maintain and restore degraded habitat, and control the spread of weedy, non-native species (USDOI 2010). Within the Santa Rosa-San Jacinto Mountains National Monument, the BLM and Forest Service aim to eradicate "noxious, non-native, and invasive" plants (USDOI and USDA 2004). The recently established San Gabriel Mountains National Monument permits the use of mechanical fuel treatment and prescribed fire where "appropriate to address the risk of wildfire, insect infestation, or disease that would endanger the objects identified above or imperil public safety" (Obama 2014).

OTHER LOCAL AND REGIONAL BENEFITS RESULTING FROM DESIGNATION

Based on the experiences in other national monuments in California, the designation of the Berryessa-Snow Mountain region as a national monument will result in an enhanced focus on forest restoration, with ensuing benefits for water quality, stream flow reliability, and prevention of catastrophic wildfires. Local residents have long sought to protect the Berryessa-Snow Mountain region in order to preserve its important scientific, recreational, and cultural values. One of the important benefits of preserving the Berryessa-Snow Mountain region is to protect water quality and supply by permanently protecting critically important headwaters of the Eel River, Stony Creek, Cache Creek, and Putah Creek, all of which provide water for a variety of downstream users; providing an increased management emphasis on water quality in the areas of origin that sustains instream and riparian resource needs for local biological and ecological processes, as well as recreational and other human uses; increasing the resilience of natural communities on the landscape to degradation by fire, which can adversely affect water quality and supply; and preventing new mining operations, which can significantly degrade water quality in a region already severely impacted by historic mining. Protecting the Berryessa-Snow Mountain landscape as a national monument designation will bring additional attention and resources to bear on the legacy mines that continue to contaminate regional water sources.

In implementing the national monument designation, attention to road placement, construction, maintenance, and removal will be a key element in the proposal, as roads are important for managing the landscape for fires, for recreation, and other purposes, but roads are also a focus of possible impacts to valued resources and concerns. Roads and motorized trails can increase wildfire occurrence. Human-ignited wildfires account for more than 90% of fires on national lands, and are almost five times more likely in areas with roads (USDA Forest Service 1996; USDA Forest Service 1998). Baxter (2004) found that vehicles can be a significant source of fire ignitions on forestlands. On the other hand, implementing fuels-management programs that help to restore fire resilience to wildlands requires access for equipment and personnel; retaining important system roads and even developing some additional roads may be an essential element in managing the monument. By preventing development of new roads that are not needed to preserve monument objects, monument designation will help prevent new fire ignitions while addressing the need for roads to fight fires that do occur.

National monument designation will enhance collaborative, cross-boundary approaches to fire management in the monument landscape, which are widely recognized in the region as benefitting private landowners as well as management agencies and the natural environment. Enhancing forest resilience to fire may result in new economic opportunities for workers in the region, for businesses in local communities, for the forest products industry, and for alternative energy enterprises. Addressing economic constraints to increasing fuels-management options in the region is an essential task for monument implementation. Designation is expected to result in increased visibility for recreational uses of federal lands, and additional funding for facility development and maintenance.

CONCLUSION

California's drought and well-understood scenarios for climate-change highlight the need to preserve the state's quality and supply of water. In addition, the health and resilience of the region's forests and other natural communities need to be protected through the development and implementation of appropriate fuels-management and fire-management approaches that are sensitive to the environmental values in this region. Permanently protecting Berryessa-Snow Mountain region through a national monument designation will help achieve water quality and supply goals by: (1) protecting headwaters of tributaries to the Eel River, Stony Creek, Cache Creek, and Putah Creek; (2) preventing water quality degradation from new mining operations; and (3) bringing additional attention and resources to bear on the remediation of legacy mines that continue to contaminate local water supplies.

Permanent protection through monument designation will help address the impacts of climate change, fire, and drought, and achieve forest health and conservation goals, by: (1) supporting and augmenting cross-boundary agency and citizen collaboration on fire management, helping to secure approvals and funding for implementing programs that improve forest health on all lands; (2) reducing excessive fine-fuels accumulations throughout the monument, particularly in forested areas, thus reducing the likelihood that ecological, recreational, economic, and other shared values on monument lands will be destroyed by fire; (3) establishing a regional conservation focus throughout the monument that can address the impacts of climate change, fire, and drought, protecting important habitat reserves throughout the monument while also enhancing regional connectivity; and (4) employing adaptive, active management of conservation lands in the monument, by using a variety of management approaches and tools to develop strategies and practices for altered future conditions caused by climate change, fire, and drought, in order to achieve desired conservation goals and conditions in monument lands.

REFERENCES

Anderson, HM, C Gaolach, J Thompson, and G Aplet. 2012. Watershed health in wilderness, roadless, and roaded areas of the National Forest system. Wilderness Society. 11 pages.

Baxter, G. 2004. Evaluating the fire ignition potential of all terrain vehicles in Alberta forests. Advantage 5(8):1-10. http://wildfire.fpinnovations.ca/40/ATVFinal.pdf (accessed 14 May 2015).

Bladon, KD, MB Emelko, U Silins, and M Stone. 2014. Wildfire and the future of water supply. Environ Sci Technol 48:8936-8943. http://pubs.acs.org/doi/abs/10.1021/es500130g (accessed 15 May 2015).

Brown, EG, Jr, California Governor. 2015. Executive Order B-29-25. http://gov.ca.gov/docs/4.1.15_Executive_Order.pdf (accessed 15 May 2015).

California Board of Forestry and Fire Protection (BOF) and California Department of Forestry and Fire Protection (CalFire). 2010. California Fire Plan. http://cdfdata.fire.ca.gov/fire_er/fpp_planning_cafireplan (accessed 15 May 2015).

California Department of Fish and Wildlife (CDFW) website: Areas of Conservation Emphasis. http://www.dfg.ca.gov/biogeodata/ace/ (accessed 14 May 2015).

California Department of Toxic Substances Control (CDTSC). 2011. Final Site Discovery Report Cache Creek Watershed: Lake, Yolo, Colusa Counties, California. California Department of Toxic Substances Control. http://tuleyome.org/pdf/Final%20Cache%20Creek%20Discovery%20Report%2012-2011.pdf (accessed 16 May 2015).

California Department of Water Resources (DWR) website: Integrated Regional Water Management. http://www.water.ca.gov/irwm/ (accessed 16 May 2015).

California Drought website. http://ca.gov/drought/ (accessed 14 May 2015).

Cayan, D, M Tyree, D Pierce, and T Das (Scripps Institution of Oceanography). 2012. Climate Change and Sea Level Rise Scenarios for California Vulnerability and Adaptation Assessment. California Energy Commission. Publication number: CEC☐500☐2012☐008. http://www.energy.ca.gov/2012publications/CEC-500-2012-008/CEC-500-2012-008.pdf (accessed 14 May 2012).

Central Valley Regional Water Quality Control Board. 2005. Staff Report, amendments to the Water Quality Control Plan for the Sacramento River and San Joaquin River Basins for the control of mercury in Cache Creek, Bear Creek, Sulphur Creek, and Harley Gulch. http://www.waterboards.ca.gov/rwqcb5/water_issues/tmdl/central_valley_projects/cache_sulphur_creek/cache_crk_hg_final_rpt_oct2005.pdf (accessed 15 May 2015).

Clinton, W. 2000. Proclamation 7295. Establishment of the Giant Sequoia National Monument. April 15, 2000.

Cook, BI, TR Ault, and JE Smerdon. 2015. Unprecedented 21st century drought risk in the American Southwest and Central Plains. Sci Adv 1:e1400082. http://advances.sciencemag.org/content/1/1/e1400082 (accessed 15 May 2015).

DellaSala, DA, JR Karr, and DM Olson. 2011. Roadless areas and clean water. J Soil Water Conserv 66(3):78A-84A. http://

www.jswconline.org/content/66/3/78A.short (accessed 15 May 2015).

Diffenbaugh, NS, DL Swain, and D Touma. 2015. Anthropogenic warming has increased drought risk in California. Proc Nat Acad Sci USA 112(13):3931-3936. http://www.pnas.org/content/112/13/3931.full (accessed 15 May 2015).

Franklin, JF, RJ Mitchell, and BJ Palik. 2007. Natural disturbance and stand development principles for ecological forestry. Gen Tech Rep NRS-19. Newtown Square, PA: USDA Forest Service, Northern Research Station. 44 p. http://courses.washington.edu/esrm315/pdfs/Franklinetal2007.pdf (accessed 17 May 2015).

Goulden, ML, and RC Bales. 2014. Mountain runoff vulnerability to increased evapotranspiration with vegetation expansion. Proc Nat Acad Sci USA 111(39):14071-14075. http://www.pnas.org/content/111/39/14071.full (accessed 16 May 2014).

Gucinski, H, MJ Furniss, RR Ziemer, and MH Brookes (ed). 2001. Forest Roads: A Synthesis of Scientific Information. Gen. Tech. Rep. PNW-GTR-509. Portland, OR: U.S. Department of Agriculture, Forest Service, Pacific Northwest Research Station. 103 p. http://www.fs.fed.us/pnw/pubs/gtr509.pdf (accessed 14 May 2015).

Halofsky, JE, DC Donato, DE Hibbs, JL Campbell, M Donaghy Cannon, JB Fontaine, JR Thompson, RG Anthony, BT Bormann, LJ Kayes, BE Law, DL Peterson, and TA Spies. 2011. Mixed-severity fire regimes: lessons and hypotheses from the Klamath-Siskiyou Ecoregion. Ecosphere 2(4):Art 40. http://www.esajournals.org/doi/abs/10.1890/ES10-00184.1 (accessed 17 May 2015).

Hannah, L, MR Shaw, M Ikegami, PR Roehrdanz, O Soong, and J Thorne. 2012. Consequences of climate change for native plants and conservation. California Energy Commission. Publication number CEC-500-2012-024. http://www.energy.ca.gov/2012publications/CEC-500-2012-024/CEC-500-2012-024.pdf (accessed 16 May 2015).

Harrison, S, and N Rajakaruna (eds). 2011. Serpentine: the evolution and ecology of a model system. Univ California Press, Berkeley, CA. 464 pages.

Intergovernmental Panel on Climate Change (IPCC). 2014. Climate Change 2014 Synthesis Report. Contribution of Working Groups I, II and III to the Fifth Assessment Report of the Intergovernmental Panel on Climate Change [Core Writing Team, R.K. Pachauri and L.A. Meyer (eds.)]. IPCC, Geneva, Switzerland, 151 pp. http://www.ipcc.ch/report/ar5/syr/ (accessed 15 May 2015).

Keeley, JE. 2002. Fire management of California shrubland landscapes. Environ Manage 29(3):395-408. http://link.springer.com/article/10.1007/s00267-001-0034-Y (accessed 16 May 2015).

Lawler, JJ, and JD Olden 2011. Reclaiming the debate over assisted colonization. Front Ecol Environ 9(10):569–574. http://www.esajournals.org/doi/pdf/10.1890/100106 (accessed 17 May 2015).

Lenihan, JM, D Bachelet, RP Neilson, and R Drapek. 2008. Response of vegetation distribution, ecosystem productivity, and fire to climate change scenarios for California. Climatic Change 87(Suppl 1):S215-S230. http://link.springer.com/article/10.1007/s10584-007-9362-0 (accessed 15 May 2015).

McKenzie, D, Z Gedalof, DL Peterson, and P Mote. 2004. Climate change, wildfire, and conservation. Conserv Biol 18:890-902. http://onlinelibrary.wiley.com/doi/10.1111/j.1523-1739.2004.00492.x (accessed 17 May 2015).

Moyle, PB, JD Kiernan, PK Crain, and RM Quiñones. 2013. Climate change vulnerability of native and alien freshwater fishes of California: a systematic assessment approach. PLoS ONE 8(5):e63883. http://journals.plos.org/plosone/article?id=10.1371/journal.pone.0063883 (accessed 16 May 2015).

Naiman, RJ, RE Bilby, and PA Bisson. 2000. Riparian ecology and management in the Pacific coastal rain forest. BioScience 50(11):996-1011. http://bioscience.oxfordjournals.org/content/50/11/996.full (accessed 16 May 2015).

National Wildlife Federation website: Climate-Smart Conservation. http://www.nwf.org/What-We-Do/Energy-and-Climate/Climate-Smart-Conservation.aspx (accessed 17 May 2015).

National Research Council. 2002. Riparian areas: functions and strategies for management. National Academy Press, Washing, DC. 436 pages. http://www.nap.edu/catalog/10327/riparian-areas-functions-and-strategies-for-management (accessed 16 May 2015).

Obama, B. 2013. Executive Order 13653: Preparing the United States for the impacts of climate change. http://www.gpo.gov/fdsys/pkg/FR-2013-11-06/pdf/2013-26785.pdf (accessed 15 May 2015).

Obama, B. 2014. Presidential Proclamation. Establishment of the San Gabriel Mountains National Monument. October 14, 2014.

Paige, G, and J Zygmunt. 2013. The science behind wildfire effects on water quality, erosion. Pages 31-34 in Living With Wildfire in Wyoming (J Thompson and SL Miller, ed.). http://www.uwyo.edu/barnbackyard/_files/documents/resources/wildfire2013/waterqualityerosion2013wywildfire.pdf (accessed 14 May 2015).

Plumb, TR. 1980. Response of oaks to fire. Pages 202-215 in: Plumb, TR (tech coord), Proceedings of the symposium on the ecology, management, and utilization of California oaks, June 26-28, 1979, Claremont, California. Gen Tech Rep PSW-144, 368 p. Pacific Southwest Forest and Range Exp Stn, Forest Serv, US Dept Agric, Berkeley, CA.

Skinner, CN, CS Abbott, DL Fry, SL Stephens, AH Taylor, and V Trouet. 2009. Human and climatic influences on fire occurrence in California's North Coast Range, USA. Fire Ecology 5(3):76-99. http://fireecologyjournal.org/docs/Journal/pdf/Volume05/Issue03/076.pdf (accessed 15 May 2015).

Sommers, WT, SG Coloff, and SG Conard. 2011. Synthesis of knowledge: fire history and climate change. Report submitted to the Joint Fire Science Program for Project 09-2-01-09. 190 pages plus 6 Appendices. http://digitalcommons.unl.edu/jfspsynthesis/19 (accessed 16 May 2015).

Spencer, WD, P Beier, K Penrod, K Winters, C Paulman, H Rustigian-Romsos, J Strittholt, M Parisi, and A Pettler. 2010. California Essential Habitat Connectivity Project: A strategy for conserving a connected California. Prepared for California Department of Transportation, California Department of Fish and Game, and Federal Highways Administration. https://www.wildlife.ca.gov/Conservation/Planning/Connectivity/CEHC (accessed 15 May 2015).

Staudt, A, AK Leidner, J Howard, KA Brauman, JS Dukes, LJ Hansen, C Paukert, J Sabo, and LA Solórzano. 2013. The added complications of climate change: understanding and managing biodiversity and ecosystems. Front Ecol Environ 11(9):494-501. http://www.esajournals.org/doi/pdf/10.1890/120275 (accessed 16 May 2015).

Stephens, SL, SW Bigelow, RD Burnett, BD Collins, CV Gallagher, J Keane, DA Kelt, MP North, LJ Roberts, PA Stine, and DH Van Vuren. 2014. California Spotted Owl, songbird, and small mammal responses to landscape fuel treatments. BioScience 64(10): 893-906. http://bioscience.oxfordjournals.org/content/early/2014/09/01/biosci.biu137.full (accessed 15 May 2015).

Stephenson, NL. 1998. Actual evapotranspiration and deficit: biologically meaningful correlates of vegetation distribution across spatial scales. J Biogeogr 25:855-870. http://onlinelibrary.wiley.com/doi/10.1046/j.1365-2699.1998.00233.x/full (accessed 16 May 2015).

Thompson, LC, and R Larsen. 2004. Fish habitat in freshwater streams. Univ Calif Agric Nat Res Publication 8112. 12 pages. http://anrcatalog.ucdavis.edu/pdf/8112.pdf (accessed 16 May 2015).

Thorne, JH, RM Boynton, LE Flint, and AL Flint. 2015. The magnitude and spatial patterns of historical and future hydrologic change in California's watersheds. Ecosphere 6:Art 24. http://dx.doi.org/10.1890/ES14-00300.1 (accessed 15 May 2015).

Taylor, AH, and CN Skinner. 2003. Mixed-severity fire regimes: lessons and hypotheses from the Klamath-Siskiyou Ecoregion. Ecol Applic 13(3):704-719. http://dx.doi.org/10.1890/1051-0761(2003)013[0704:SPACOH]2.0.CO;2 (accessed 17 May 2015).

Troendle, CA, and WK Olsen. 1994. Potential effects of timber harvest and water management on streamflow dynamics and sediment transport. Pages 34-41 in: Covington, WW, and LF DeBano (tech. coord.), Sustainable ecological systems: implementing an ecological approach to land management. 1993 July 12-15; Flagstaff, Arizona. Gen. Tech. Rep. RM-247. Fort Collins, CO: U.S. Department of Agriculture, Forest Service, Rocky Mountain Forest and Range Experiment Station.

USDA Forest Service. 1995. Mendocino National Forest Land and Resource Management Plan.

USDA Forest Service. 1996. National Forest Fire Report, 1994. Washington DC.

USDA Forest Service. 1998. 1991-1997 Wildland Fire Statistics. Fire and Aviation Management, Washington, D.C.

USDA Forest Service. 2001. Roadless Area Conservation Rule Preamble (Federal Register .Vol. 66, No. 9. January 12, 2001. Pages 3245-3247) and Final Environmental impact Statement Final Environmental Impact Statement, Vol. 1, 3–3 to 3–7.

USDA Forest Service. 2012. Giant Sequoia National Monument Management Plan. http://www.fs.usda.gov/Internet/FSE_DOCUMENTS/stelprd3797629.pdf (accessed 15 May 2015).

USDA Forest Service, Pacific Southwest Region (Region 5). 2013. Ecological Restoration Implementation Plan. R5-MB-249. http://www.fs.usda.gov/detail/r5/landmanagement/?cid=stelprdb5409054 (accessed 14 May 2015).

USDA Rocky Mountain Research Station. 2011. Wildfire effects on erosion and stream water. National Fire Plan Research Highlight. http://www.fs.fed.us/rm/science-application-integration/docs/national-fire-plan/wildfire-effects.pdf (accessed 14 May 2015).

USDOI Bureau of Land Management, USDA Forest Service. 2004. Santa Rosa and San Jacinto Mountains National Monument Final Management Plan and Record of Decision. February 2004.

USDOI Bureau of Land Management. 2010. Carrizo Plain National Monument Approved Resource Management Plan and Record of Decision. February 2010.

USEPA Western Ecology Division website: Level III and IV Ecoregions of the Continental United States. http://www.epa.gov/wed/pages/ecoregions/level_iii_iv.htm (accessed 17 May 2015).

US Fish and Wildlife Service. 2011. Revised Recovery Plan for the Northern Spotted Owl (Strix occidentalis caurina). US Fish and Wildlife Service, Portland, Oregon. xvi + 258 pp. http://www.fws.gov/ecos/ajax/docs/recovery_plan/NSO%20Final%20Rec%20Plan%20051408.pdf (accessed 15 May 2015).

van Mantgem, PJ, NL Stephenson, JC Byrne, LD Daniels, JF Franklin, PZ Fulé, ME Harmon, AJ Larson, JM Smith, AH Taylor, and TT Veblen. 2009. Widespread increase of tree mortality rates in the western United States. Science 323:521-524. http://www.sciencemag.org/content/323/5913/521.full (accessed 15 May 2015).

Westerling, AL, B.P Bryant, HK Preisler, TP Holmes, HG Hidalgo, T Das, and SR Shrestha. 2011. Climate change and growth scenarios for California wildfire. Climatic Change 109(Suppl 1):S445-S463. http://link.springer.com/article/10.1007/s10584-011-0329-9 (accessed 15 May 2015).

Made in United States
Orlando, FL
25 January 2023